425
425

WORKING STEAM

261
261
261
AURORA
POLICE

WORKING STEAM

Vintage Locomotives Today

Hans Halberstadt

MetroBooks

MetroBooks

An Imprint of Friedman/Fairfax Publishers

Library of Congress Cataloging-in-Publication Data available upon request

ISBN 1-56799-776-7

Editor: Ann Kirby
Art Director: Kevin Ullrich
Designer: Kevin Ullrich and Jonathan Gaines
Photography Editor: Sarah Storey
Production Manager: Camille Lee

Color separations by HK Scanner Arts Int'l Ltd.
Printed and bound in China by Leefung-Asco Printers Ltd.

10 9 8 7 6 5 4 3 2 1

For bulk purchases and special sales, please contact:
Friedman/Fairfax Publishers
Attention: Sales Department
15 West 26th Street
New York, NY 10010
212/685-6610 FAX 212/685-1307

Visit our website:
http://www.metrobooks.com

TITLE PAGE:

All steamed up, with someplace to go, Steamtown's refurbished Baldwin switcher No. 26 simmers quietly at the beginning of a new career.

CONTENTS PAGE:

Jupiter awaits orders at Promontory, Utah, on the very spot where the rails were joined in May 1869.

DEDICATION

For my son, John Sterling Halberstadt

ACKNOWLEDGMENTS

A salute and thanks to all the nice folks who helped put this consist on track and on schedule:

Howard Ande

Al Broadfoot, BC Rail

Lou Chiramonte, Niles Canyon Railway

Glen Christofferson

Bob Dowty, Golden Spike National Historic Site

Aarne Frobom, Michigan Trust for Historic Railway Preservation

Michael Green

Erik Halberstadt, researcher

Steve Lee, Union Pacific Steam Program

Tom Lund, Kalmbach Publications

Mike Mangini and Ray Brown, Project 2472

Ken Prager, Portland Railroad Preservation Association

Dan Ranger, Roaring Camp & Big Trees

Steve Sandberg, North Star Rail

Brian Solomon

Don Wheeler, Portland Railroad Preservation Association

Kyle Wyatt, Curator of History, State of Nevada

Contents

Preface

This is the saga of a steam-powered success strategy. Over the past two or three decades, North Americans have become very interested in historic preservation generally, and with the preservation of railroad resources specifically. Without a lot of fanfare, an awesome number of people—both individuals and groups—have been restoring and preserving buildings, artifacts, and even steam locomotives. While some of us are lamenting the passing of grand old machines, others are busy salvaging them, firing them up, and taking them for rides.

The age of steam power on main line railroads ended about forty years ago. It is true that thousands of glorious steam locomotives fell, like iron dinosaurs, to the cutting torch. But it is also true that many were saved.

About fourteen hundred steamers, of all sizes and types, exist in Canada and the United States today. Of those, an amazing three hundred or so are still operational. Tiny little switchers by the dozens, at least ten giant 4-8-4 Northerns, and even a huge 4-6-6-4 Challenger are still in business, running the rails. Union Pacific Railroad, whose corporate history was powered by steam, has never retired one of its big, old locomotives, No. 844, and still puts it in rare revenue service. Best of all, some of

the engines parked in playgrounds and other public places as static displays are now being brought back to joyous life and put back on track.

Steam power is alive and well at the dawn of the twenty-first century. Although some wonderful steam locomotives have been recently retired—Norfolk Southern's glorious streamlined Number 611 in particular—others have been resurrected. While some old locomotives have been run into the ground, worked until the drivers nearly fell off the axles, others are getting complete rebuilds. Nobody is cutting up locomotives anymore. Some folks say that Norfolk Southern's newly retired 611 is just taking a rest before running again.

Owners and operators of steam locomotives have begun to look beyond mere

Sierra Railroad's No. 28 is a working engine, appearing often in Hollywood films and regularly hauling tourist trains through the old Gold Rush foothills of California.

preservation of old iron. Instead of doing the minimum amount of work to make a locomotive serviceable, today operators are investing huge sums in total rebuilds to keep their locomotives steamed up for twenty or thirty more years. This is a surprising and encouraging development.

The skills, the machine tools, the parts, and the will to bring a massive steam locomotive back to factory-fresh condition still exist. Grand Canyon Railway in Arizona and Valley Railroad in Connecticut have both recently completed comprehensive overhauls on their Mikado locomotives. BC Rail of Canada has done the same for its Royal Hudson. Each of these renovated locomotives is still a hard-working, profit-generating machine, today as in the past.

This book is about the present and future of steam, not its dead past. It is a survey of just a few of the many steam locomotives currently in operation in the United States and Canada. In fact, there are too many locomotive operations even to list in a book like this. A representative list of selected railroad museums, operational short lines, and steam locomotive preservation groups can be found at the back of this volume, but a complete list would be a book in itself.

BLUE MO
B & REA
TH   DWIN LOCOMOTIVE
26

Getting Up Steam

One of the unsung virtues of older age is that experience provides memories of events that younger people can now only read about and try to imagine. I am just old enough to recall the very end of working steam locomotives, and my memories are clear and bright.

Back in the 1950s, when I was just a wee lad, my folks bought a house on a hill overlooking a branch line of the Northern Pacific Railroad. Twice a week or so, a small locomotive—a 2-8-0 most likely—chuffed up the right-of-way. A tiny consist of perhaps a half-dozen cars rattled along from the San Francisco Bay town of Sausalito bound for Mill Valley at the other end of a very short line. The sight of that little engine—its drivers flashing with a musical tempo, its white banner of steam on high, moving purposefully across my young field of view—was a thrilling, beautiful, and eternally memorable sight.

It was too good to last. One week the flashing locomotive was suddenly gone, replaced with a funny-looking shoe box of a machine. The diesel locomotive had arrived, not with a bang but a whimper. This new locomotive had no flash, no glorious banner. There was nothing at all to thrill my senses. Steam trains disappeared from my personal world sometime about

*I*nterior view **(left)** *of the National Park Service's grand new railroad museum, Steamtown, in Scranton, Pennsylvania.* **ABOVE:** *Venting steam from a cylinder.*

1953. I didn't know it then, but steam locomotives were also disappearing in much the same way from the rails across North America and the rest of the world. Everywhere, dozens of giant and nearly new state-of-the-art engines, the Northern, Challenger, Consolidation, Big Boy—impossibly huge machines, incredibly powerful, fast, and reliable—came out of scheduled service. It happened almost all at once. Those massive boilers, designed to operate at three hundred pounds (136kg) of pressure and at eight hundred degrees Fahrenheit (427°C), suddenly cooled. Those glittering drivers were allowed to rust. The once-proud technology which had moved most cargo and many travelers around North America had suddenly become obsolete.

The steamers were pulled from service as quickly as diesel locomotives could be manufactured to replace them. Steam locomotives that had been sold for a princely sum of a quarter-million dollars

nearly new were now sold for scrap. They were drawn, quartered, and butchered by the dozens, hundreds, and thousands. In some cases, every single example of a class of locomotive fell to the cutting torch.

The passing of these workhorses was lamented by almost everybody—everybody but the accountants at the railroads. The diesel wasn't nearly as powerful as the steamer, or as fast, or as dependable. At the time, diesels were weak compared to more powerful steam power. Only during the last few years has a diesel engine equaled the power of the biggest steamers.

Instead, the diesel offered something the railroads couldn't ignore: tremendous economy. A steamer needs constant care and attention, and it needs water and fuel every one hundred miles (161km). A diesel goes much farther before it needs to refuel, and it never needs water. Although a single diesel couldn't begin to offer the same drawbar power of an equivalent steamer, multiple diesels could be connected as a powerful lash-up, controlled from the cab of the lead engine.

The earliest practical diesel-electric locomotives first went into yard service as switchers during the 1920s, then into fast main line passenger service in the 1930s, and finally proved themselves in the World War II years of the early 1940s. As soon as the war was over, so was the practical age of railroad steam.

But steam locomotion didn't quite become extinct. Some railroads preserved a few locomotives for sentimental reasons. Norfolk Southern ran occasional steam excursions for their public relations value until recently, and Union Pacific still fires up its vintage steamers.

Southern Pacific donated its steam locomotives to just about any community that wanted one. Museums claimed as many old locomotives as they could store. A few individuals even bought them for scrap value, then put them on display.

So while thousands of grand steam locomotives were scrapped, many others have been preserved. There are about two thousand locomotives in North America today, several hundred in running condition. You can still visit, watch, ride in, and, in some cases, actually learn to operate steam locomotives at sites in the United States and Canada, proving that the steam locomotive is still alive and well.

Steamtown's switcher (below) is a veteran of the Baldwin Locomotive works and Jackson Iron and Steel Company. Built in March 1929, the locomotive labored in the massive Eddystone Locomotive Works for many years.
PRECEDING PAGES: *Sierra Railroad's oil-fired Baldwin ten-wheeler cautiously backs out of the old Jamestown roundhouse into a chilly winter morning.*

Locomotive Jams and Preserves

Union Pacific's Steve Lee describes conflicts between locomotive preservationists.

People have different ideas about how steam locomotives ought to be preserved. While nearly all rail fans and most of the public want their locomotives steamed up and moving, a substantial number of museum and curatorial professionals are highly critical of such efforts.

Steve Lee runs a unique steam program and a unique steam locomotive. The program is Union Pacific's very ambitious and expensive attempt to keep its rich heritage of railroad history vital. It does that by keeping a huge 4-6-6-4 Challenger and a 4-8-4 Northern locomotive alive. Only one Challenger remains functional, although many others in Union Pacific's collection are on static display. Lee and others who believe steam locomotives need to be run to be appreciated fight occasional battles with curators who want steam locomotives preserved in showroom condition inside museums. Steve explains the conflict:

We have quite a conflict with some of the professional preservationists. The outlook of some of these people is that we ought to be shot or hung for operating historic steam locomotives. These people, who write and lecture about locomotives, but who would never get their hands dirty with a wrench, tell us that we are destroying historic artifacts by operating them. They seem to think that locomotives like the Challenger and No. 844 ought to be disassembled, meticulously documented, then reassembled and stored in a controlled environment— "stuffed and mounted" for people to see.

Well, most of the steam locomotives that still exist are stuffed and mounted in a park or a museum. But seeing a cold, dead, lifeless object does not tell you much about a steam locomotive. A steam locomotive is a collection of sights, smells, sounds—it is the ground shaking and the flash of the drivers as it goes by!

So we reject the notion that we're desecrating these historic artifacts. You can learn some things about locomotives by looking at one in a museum, but you can't tell what they were unless you can see one, out running down the rails.

Inside the remains of the old, refurbished Delaware, Lackawanna & Western roundhouse, Baldwin No. 26 gets a little attention from one of the Steamtown crew.

Chapter 1

A Short History of Steam

All locomotives are interesting machines. The entire motive power system of the locomotive and of railroad transportation defies common sense, if you think about it: a smooth, polished steel wheel rides on an equally smooth, polished steel rail; the area of actual contact between the rail and each wheel is tiny, only the size of a quarter, perhaps a square inch (6.5 sq. cm) or so.

The locomotive is extremely heavy, and with the additional load of trailing cars, the total often represents thousands of tons of dead-weight inertia. When power is applied to the locomotive wheels, common sense indicates that they ought to spin like car tires on ice.

That's exactly what early railroad designers thought would happen. Instead, the locomotive's weight produces adhesion between the wheel and rail. The heavier the weight, the greater the adhesion.

The American steam locomotive was first imported from Britain and has no single inventor. In England, a tiny locomotive called Puffing Billy was at work as early as 1813, hauling coal wagons in Northumberland. Just a few years later, in 1821, the British Parliament authorized construction of the first railroad line. Named the Stockton & Darlington Railway, it was in business by 1825.

Locomotives used on these first lines were quite light and simple. Even so,

Virginia & Truckee No. 29 (left) is pretty typical of the kind of locomotive that did most of the work, most of the time during the steam era. **ABOVE:** *Detail of Baltimore & Ohio "Tom Thumb" replica.*

steam locomotive inventor George Stephenson's engine, named the Locomotion, managed to haul a mixed consist of cargo and 450 passengers, a load estimated at thirty tons (27t), for a distance of almost nine miles (14.5km) at an average speed of about 8mph (13kph) on its first run.

Today that performance might not seem impressive, but it was considered amazing for its time. Within a few years, railroads were in operation all over the British Isles, running on beautifully designed roadbeds, lavishly funded by public and private sources, and powered by four- and six-wheeled locomotives.

North American efforts at establishing a railroad began in 1829—initiated using four imported British locomotives. Roadbeds in North America were rough, often steep, and twisting, hacked out of the wilderness, across a rugged landscape. The imported British engines, with stiff frames and large drivers, derailed easily, brutalizing both the track and the crew. Despite the problems, the idea of a railroad captured the imagination of the public in the 1830s, and demand for new lines—and the equipment to operate them—became intense. The British engines were adapted to North American rails, and North American locomotive industry began to evolve.

The essential modification in locomotive design for North America came along in 1832, when John Jervis introduced a swiveling four-wheel leading truck to a locomotive with two driving wheels at the rear. The leading truck and resultant three-point suspension provided a tremendous improvement—a much more stable ride and less likelihood of derailing. This pioneering engine was initially christened the Experiment, then rebuilt and renamed Brother Jonathan. With only two drivers, this type of engine had very poor track adhesion and its tractive power was quite limited.

A second set of driving wheels was added in 1835, with dramatic results in performance. It was a locomotive wheel layout that would dominate North American railroads for the rest of the century and later became known as the American or American Standard pattern.

LOCOMOTIVE PRODUCTION

Demand for railroad locomotives greatly exceeded North American steam engine manufacturing capability. To fill the need, English locomotives were imported by the dozen. But the tremendous demand, along with the specialized roadbed requirements of the North American terrain, soon produced a new industry.

In 1835, North American builders produced thirty-five new locomotives, based on English designs. A decade later, about two hundred shiny new locomotives had joined the older iron horses in the sta-

*Norfolk & Western's No. 1218 (**left**) was one of fifteen 2-6-6-4 locomotives built during the frantic days of 1943. The last of them didn't retire until 1961, and this one was still working the excursion trade in 1987.*

*Detail of the little Tom Thumb reproduction locomotive (**above**).*

They don't come much smaller than this Falk No.1 (opposite), a little logging locomotive from the deep woods of Northern California. The whole locomotive weighs just ten tons (9t), less than the leading trucks on many locomotives. Even so, it hauled huge redwood logs from 1883 until 1928.

ble, and virtually none were imported. Although a few were still based on the old British wheel pattern, the majority were 4-4-0 American Standard machines. A great network of rails began to stitch together isolated communities, changing North American society forever.

One firm quickly dominated this industry from the beginning: the Baldwin Company, founded by Matthias W. Baldwin. Baldwin contributed fourteen new locomotives in 1835, almost half of all the American locomotives produced that year. Baldwin expanded production, and in 1860 the company built eighty-three new engines. Baldwin had stiff competition: about six hundred new locomotives went into service that year. Baldwin's total for 1870 was 280; it went to 517 a decade later. By the turn of the century, Baldwin was producing more than twelve hundred

new locomotives annually, about 40 percent of the total American production. By 1900, more than seventeen thousand Baldwin locomotives were in service in North America, in addition to other Baldwin engines shipped abroad. Sheer production volume is one reason the Baldwin name dominates among the ranks of locomotive survivors.

STANDARDIZATION

Rapid and prolific locomotive production was necessary to serve the vast expanses of the North American continent. From east to west, new railroads were being chartered as quickly as they could be organized. American locomotive builders quickly decided that the best way to keep up with demand was to offer a basic model with as many elements standardized as possible. Although efforts to standardize locomotive

design began as early as 1831, the first accepted standard machine was the 4-4-0, invented in 1835 and eventually christened the American Standard in 1870.

Another design that became an industry-wide standard, the 4-6-0—known as the Mogul—appeared in the 1850s, offering enhanced traction and the ability to haul heavier trains. By the 1880s, these new, bigger locomotives—with six drivers, bigger fireboxes, and more steaming capacity—were replacing the original 4-4-0 American Standard locomotives.

In May 1869, the transcontinental rail link across the United States was completed, with the Canadian link following in 1885, and the web of rails soon expanded across the western continent. Farms and cities appeared all across the prairies and the West, all dependent on the railroad for transportation of people and goods. As a

Kettle Moraine No. 9 (**above**) is a featured performer at Kettle Moraine Railway, in North Lake, Wisconsin.

Typical of many of the locomotives lost to the cutting torch, Chicago, Burlington & Quincy's No. 5100 (**right**) rots quietly on a back track in August 1956.

result, freight and passenger traffic boomed during the last two decades of the nineteenth century. Larger locomotives were introduced, totally dwarfing the old standard Americans and Moguls.

GROWING PAINS

Growth of the North American rail network was explosive in the years leading up to the American Civil War, nearly all of it based on the 4-4-0 locomotive. But as traffic demands increased, and as the quality of roadbeds improved, larger locomotives became practical.

The first little locomotives, like the Brother Jonathan of 1832, weighed about fourteen thousand pounds (6,350kg) and were sixteen to twenty feet (4.9–6.1m) long; the boilers operated at around 50 psi. These engines could generate about one thousand pounds (454kg) of tractive effort.

Over the next century, as steam technology improved and the rails and roadbeds became stronger and smoother, locomotives of tremendous power and speed evolved. By the turn of the century, the American Standard 4-4-0 was fifty-seven feet long (17.4m), weighed more than 200,000 pounds (90,800kg), and could pull a train at more than 110 mph (177kph).

At about the same time, 4-6-2 Moguls had pretty well displaced the American Standard. The extra set of drivers allowed a much bigger firebox, which produced more steam from a longer boiler. More steam meant higher speeds with better endurance and tractive effort.

Since locomotive width and height were limited by existing bridges, tunnels, and track gauge, the only way to make bigger boilers for more powerful locomotives was to make them longer. The trend toward longer engines began in 1903, with the Mallet articulated locomotive frame and compound steam engines. The compound engine, a system that recycles steam through a sequence of pistons, worked well on ships but was too bulky and heavy for

Not all locomotives were designed for drawbar work. This logging locomotive used its power to operate a winch.

locomotives. The hinged frame and multiple sets of drivers worked quite well, though, and soon became popular in parts of the United States and Canada.

Around World War I, locomotives grew into giants, designed to haul scores of fully loaded coal and iron ore gondolas. The Consolidation, Mikado, Pacific, Atlantic, and other fast, powerful locomotive models completely displaced the older and smaller Mogul, American Standard, and ten-wheeler.

After World War I, two types of locomotives dominated the rails. One was the enormous freight locomotive of the Texas type, with two wheels on the leading truck and ten drivers, plus another four on the trailing truck. These engines were designed for very heavy trains. The other locomotive type was designed for speed, featuring larger drivers and huge boilers. It was meant for passenger service and express freight, particularly cross-country shipment of perishables. The massive Northern class is an example. It appeared in 1926—739,000 pounds (335,500kg), more than 6,100 pounds (2,770kg) of tractive effort—in a package 105 feet (32m) long.

Then in the 1930s, several classes of engine appeared with machines weighing more than one million pounds (454,000kg). The Challenger class was one of these, with locomotives 121 feet (37m) long, steam

Colorado & Southern's No. 9, (above) tricked out with a small snowplow, is a narrow-gauge 2-6-0, built by Cooke in 1884. FOLLOWING PAGES: *Pacific-class 4-6-2 locomotives were built in many shapes and sizes, but most looked a lot like this handsome version from Baldwin, at a halt near Port Jervis, New York.*

B.M.&R.
425
BLUE MOUNTAIN
B&READING
BLUE MOUNTAIN
B&READING
AT 425

425
425
425

pressure of 280 pounds (127kg), and 97,400 pounds (44,220kg) of tractive effort.

DEBUT OF THE DIESEL

The diesel locomotive made its American debut in 1924. At first it was a weak, ugly, slow, and homely little creature, relegated strictly to switching duties. Kept in the background, the diesel-electric was scarcely noticed by the public or by railroad professionals. Railroad accountants and designers noticed, though. What they saw was a technology that required very little maintenance, that seldom needed fuel, and that worked around the clock.

The American Locomotive Company (ALCO), a longtime major supplier of steam locomotives, jumped into diesel technology early with a turbocharged nine-hundred-horsepower four-stroke-cycle unit. General Motors also made the leap with its competing two-stroke-cycle diesel designed for railroad use. In 1934, GM built its Zephyr, a complete train that showcased the new technology. It was an odd-looking, stainless steel, shovel-nosed unit that hummed instead of roared. The streamlined diesel locomotive, with its trail of stainless steel cars, flashed across the Midwest from Denver to Chicago, seldom stopping. Suddenly steam technology looked old-fashioned, and diesel technology looked modern.

Until recently, diesel locomotives were never as powerful as the most powerful steam engines. These power units are, however, "modular" and capable of being coupled together into what engineers call lash-ups, which are able to meet any power requirement. The conversion to diesel power began almost immediately.

THE END OF THE LINE

World War II slowed the conversion trend, and many steam locomotives were still built during the war. After wartime fuel restrictions were lifted, diesels began replacing steam locomotives all across North America. Diesels were clearly cheaper to operate per ton-mile of cargo hauled, and so it was the accountants who wrote the final chapter of main line steam.

Diesel and steam coexisted for about fifteen years. In some ways, those years were the high point of steam locomotive design and operation—huge engines blasting across the continent during the war years, and for a while afterward. The builders experimented with new technology—a steam turbine was put into service—but the diesel's economic virtues overwhelmed all objections.

*This tiny 0-4-0 tank engine (**far left**) survives as a static display near where it labored, in Guadalajara, Mexico.* **LEFT:** *Southern Pacific's No. 4449 is one of the most popular and beloved surviving steamers. Based in Portland, Oregon, she has delighted thousands during her occasional excursions up and down the West Coast.*

CHAPTER 2

Anatomy of a Steam Locomotive

Steam locomotives are strange, mysterious, lifelike creatures encumbered with all sorts of warts, limbs, lumps, tubes, and unknown components. But most steam locomotives—big and small, ancient and modern—share the same basic anatomy and work in a similar way.

Water is heated in a closed vessel and evaporated into steam; the steam is pressurized, then released through a valve to move a piston. The piston turns a wheel, and the wheel moves the locomotive down the track. That's it. But a look at any locomotive reveals a confusing maze of components: pipes, levers, domes, and all sorts of objects that defy identification. Here's a short course in steam locomotive anatomy.

BOILER

The real fuel used by a steam locomotive isn't coal, wood, or oil, but steam itself. The locomotive's power depends entirely upon its ability to produce steam in the large volumes required to move a heavy train. This requirement has been the foundation for the primary specification of most locomotive designs.

The boiler itself is almost always a horizontal cylinder, from ten to nearly one hundred feet (3–30m) in length. Inside the cylinder, at the back, is the firebox, a box

*The right side driving wheels, side rods, and main rod (**left**) of a typical 4-6-0 locomotive, ready to roll.*
ABOVE: *This handsome brass throttle is installed in a little geared Shay.*

within a tin can, the furnace where heat is generated. This firebox may be wide and shallow if the locomotive is designed for burning anthracite coal, or narrow and deep for burning wood or bituminous coal. The fuel rests on a grate through which air can flow. The heat and combustion products flow from the firebox through horizontal boiler tubes forward to the front of the boiler to the smoke box, then out through the stack. All these tubes and the firebox itself are surrounded by water, and the heat from the fire quickly heats the water.

Boilers are designed to transmit as much heat to the water as possible. The boiler looks like it might be full of water, but in fact it is mostly dry. The space between the sides of the firebox, for example, and the boiler is only two to four inches (5–10.1cm) in most locomotives. The result of all this is a very large area of sheet metal heated by the fire, with a fairly small quantity of water in close contact with the hot metal.

RIGHT: *Pare Marquette No. 1225 simmers patiently before a run out of St. Charles, Michigan. The boiler is mostly full of fire and steam, not water; it is typically made of steel plate, artfully formed and assembled, and able to contain hundreds of pounds of pressure.*
OPPOSITE: *The cab of any locomotive contains a bewildering assortment of controls and instruments. The fundamentals, though, are simple: throttle, "Johnson bar," controls for the airbrake and engine brakes, steam pressure gauge, air pressure gauge.*

Now, the term *small* is relative. A moderate-sized locomotive may have a boiler capacity of about fifty-five hundred gallons (20,820l) of water. That may sound like a lot—until you think of it as only ten fifty-five-gallon (208l) drums. Most of the boiler, then, is full of fire, not water.

But the boiler uses up water at a great rate during normal operations, and even standing still. As that water evaporates, it must be replaced—and that's not a simple process because the interior is pressurized to between about 70psi and 300psi. The water has to be forced in.

Originally, and on some old 4-4-0 American Standard locomotives, that was done with a pump, usually attached to the piston crosshead. But for the past hundred years and more, most locomotives employ an injector to do the job. This device uses the velocity of released steam in a venturi chamber to force the water past a check valve and into the boiler.

Another mystery device found on many locomotives is a feed water heater. Rather than add cold water to a hot boiler, thus cooling the boiler down, steam engine designers started using waste heat going up the stack to preheat the water before pumping it inside. Feed water heaters are usually pretty obvious if you know what to look for—a big cylinder just in front of the stack, or an inverted U-shaped device on the front of the smoke-box door.

FIREBOX

Airflow is important to any fire. Without positive ventilation, the fire in the firebox would quickly go out. Very early in the development of steam technology, exhaust steam from the cylinders was used to suck air into the firebox, making the firebox into a blast furnace. In virtually all steam loco-motives, exhaust steam from the cylinders is routed to a venturi in the smokestack. The effect of the blast of steam through

T*he sound of the steam whistle quickly captures the imagination of anybody who hears it. They were made in many shapes and sizes, each with a very distinctive sound. This little example's cheerful tweet echos off the hills surrounding Roaring Camp's line.*

this venturi pulls huge volumes of air into the firebox, sucking heat and smoke through the boiler tubes and out of the stack. This blast of air can actually lift the fire right off the grate on some engines, when running hard.

One of the major improvements to locomotives was the Wooten firebox. These are quite evident in most locomotives; they are extremely wide and angled at the sides, just forward of the cab. Wooten fireboxes use the maximum allowable width of the locomotive for a grate designed for maximum surface area. Coal is distributed

across this surface in a thin layer, allowing maximum contact with inlet air.

STEAM DOME

Most locomotives have at least two domes on top of the boiler. One of these, usually toward the rear, is the steam dome. Here the steam is collected, high above the surface of the water, where it is hottest and driest. A large tube—the dry pipe—collects the steam and carries it back down to the valves and cylinders. The whistle is typically mounted onto the steam dome, along with one or more safety valves. These spring-loaded devices open and release steam if the pressure exceeds a maximum safe level—a major embarrassment to the fireman who is expected never to let that happen.

SAND DOME

Virtually all locomotives use sand for added traction, supplied from a reservoir on top of the boiler. This supply is usually in a dome that looks almost identical to the steam dome. The sand dome is generally the first one behind the smokestack and will often have a tube running from its base down to an outlet in front of the driving wheels. Some locomotives have two sand domes, particularly the very long Mallet types and other extremely powerful models of the late steam era.

Locomotives designed to work in slippery conditions—on wet or icy mountain grades, for example—typically have huge sand reservoirs with capacities of up to two thousand pounds (908kg).

Piston rod, crosshead, and valve gear. The small cylinders are lubricators designed to keep all the sliding surfaces well oiled and greased.

———

CYLINDERS AND VALVING

The actual engine part of a locomotive is quite simple mechanically. A reciprocating piston fits in a cylinder. Steam under pressure is admitted by a valve first to one side of the piston, pushing it to the end of its travel. A rod attached to the center of the piston is attached directly to one of the driving wheels through a linkage. That driving rod turns the wheel, which moves the locomotive.

Toward the end of the piston's stroke, steam pressure is cut off to that side of the piston; then the valve opens and supplies steam to the other side of the piston, pushing it back in the other direction.

The valve is designed to exhaust one side of the piston while it is pressurizing the other. The result is a piston that is working on every stroke. That's quite different from a conventional gasoline internal combustion engine, which works on only one stroke of every four.

Cylinders and valve housings are usually horizontal castings mounted at the front of the locomotive. Some of them are incredibly large—twenty-eight-inch (71cm) bores and thirty-inch (76cm) strokes or even larger on bigger locomotives of the late steam era.

RUNNING GEAR

One end of the piston rod is attached to a massive link called the main rod; the other end connects to one of the driving wheels, transmitting the power from the piston's back-and-forth motion to the rotary motion of the wheels. Side rods link the driving wheels together, transmitting the piston's power to all drivers.

Drivers on most locomotives are four to seven feet (1.2–2.1m) in diameter, cast iron or steel, with replaceable steel rims called tires. These tires are usually (but not always) flanged to stay on the track and are reground at regular intervals to ensure each driver is both perfectly circular and of equal diameter.

FRAME AND SUSPENSION

Frames were originally made of wood and wrought iron bolted together, but by about 1850, frames were typically constructed from fabricated iron. Later, toward the end of the nineteenth century, they would be cast iron. In the golden age of steam, in the years following World War I, even the largest locomotive frames were monster castings made of steel. Small switching locomotives have iron or steel frames about two inches (5cm) thick; the largest and heaviest are about four to six inches (10.1–15.3cm) thick.

American locomotives have always used some kind of suspension system to allow individual drivers to maintain contact with our notoriously uneven rails. On most steam locomotives, this involves slots and bearings in the frame that permit the driver axle to rise and fall several inches.

CONTROLS

Locomotive cabs seem to be as complex as modern transport aircraft cockpits, and so they are. There are dozens of controls for many major and minor systems on the engine. The four basic controls are the throttle, the engine brake, the train line air brake, and the "Johnson bar" or reverse lever.

The throttle operates a simple linkage that opens the valve at the top of the steam dome, regulating the volume of steam sent to the cylinders.

The Johnson bar controls the position of the valve feeding steam to the cylinders. By adjusting this control, the engineer can deliver full pressure to the cylinder for its entire stroke or for just a portion of the stroke. A full measure delivers full power but wastes steam; it also makes the locomotive bark in a loud, pleasing way that

Another look at the piston rod and its associated hardware. The squarish box on top of the cylinder is the valve assembly, feeding steam to both sides of the piston; every stroke in a steam engine is a power stroke.

Boiler Explosions

A look at the potential dangers at working with steam power.

Boiler explosions have been rare but dramatic events in the evolution of steam locomotive technology. The earliest British and American engines, back in the early 1800s, had a bad habit of detonating at unexpected moments, generally with fatal results. But within a few years, train crews learned enough about steam technology safety procedures to keep the explosions to a minimum. Even so, they were and still are a major hazard.

Here's the problem: there really isn't a lot of water in the boiler, just a few inches surrounding lots of sheet metal that is exposed to temperatures up to two thousand degrees Fahrenheit (1100°C). A big locomotive like a Northern, running hard, can evaporate four gallons (15l) of water every second. There are only a few inches of water covering the so-called crown sheet at the top of the firebox, and that level drops fast unless the fireman pays close attention to the water-level indicator glass on the rear of the boiler. His job is to keep the water level within close limits, under varying conditions, and with an indicator that is often very difficult to read.

Very rarely, the fireman misreads the gauge or neglects his duties and the water level drops far enough to expose the crown sheet. When that happens, the two-thousand-degree fire in the furnace quickly turns the sheet metal red—then white—hot. If the crew fails to notice the problem, or if the built-in safety device fails to work, the crown sheet will fail. The results can be spectacular.

When the crown sheet fails, all the pressure in the boiler is suddenly released in a fraction of a second. All the heat energy in the water—normally at temperatures far above the atmospheric boiling point—is suddenly released. All the water in the boiler evaporates in a fraction of a second, expands to many times its previous volume, and escapes through the broken crown sheet.

The amount of energy released this way is tremendous. When it happens, even on huge locomotives of the biggest classes, the entire boiler is typically ripped from the frame and tossed high in the air, end over end. In one case, the boiler flew off the locomotive frame and rocketed down the track for half a mile.

The effects on the crew are instantaneous and fatal.

Of course, there are safety devices and procedures to prevent this from ever occurring. At the top of the crown sheet is a fusible plug made of soft metal, designed to melt at fairly low temperatures. If the crown sheet is exposed and allowed to heat to eight hundred degrees (427°C) or so, this plug melts long before the sheet steel of the firebox can fail. Then all the steam in the boiler vents through the plug hole, right into the fire, putting it out almost instantly. The locomotive is out of action, and the crew will probably be out of work, but no lives will be lost or locomotives destroyed. Train crews are very careful about avoiding boiler explosions.

*It takes a while for the guages (**right**) to come off the pin as the boiler slowly warms. Engineer and fireman both consult the guages often during operations, using them as a guide for both safety and economy.*

hotshot "hoggers" enjoy. But most of the time the engineer will set the Johnson bar in the "company notch," a setting that economizes fuel and water.

ACCESSORIES

All locomotives, since very early times, have installed accessories for safety and crew comfort. The bell and whistle are both safety accessories, and so is the headlight. As locomotives grew in size, the size and number of accessories also grew. Following are the basic ones.

Generator

Early locomotives used headlights with coal oil lamps for illumination, but by the late 1800s, electrical lamps began to replace them. These lamps used batteries for power, but soon enough generators were added to provide a more reliable power source. Locomotives built since 1900 are likely to have two such generators, often mounted just forward of the cab and powered by a small steam turbine. The output of these generators is pretty weak, just enough to power the headlight and cab illumination.

Air Compressor

Air brakes are now mandatory on virtually all locomotives. Pressure for the brake pipe is supplied from a compressor and reservoir on the locomotive. The compressor is found on the left side of most steam locomotives and is operated by steam pressure.

Feed Water Heater

Another accessory added to locomotives around the turn of the century is the feed water heater. This device resembles either a large cylinder or horseshoe and is usually mounted just forward of the stack. It uses waste heat going up the stack to preheat water before injection to the boiler.

Automatic Stoker

Although not very visible from outside the cab, large coal-fired locomotives have automatic stokers to feed fuel to the firebox. These were invented out of necessity when locomotives became so large that one man couldn't keep up with the firebox's appetite for coal, no matter how fast he shoveled. Typical automatic stokers are sometimes visible as large tubes connecting the tender and rear of the locomotive, below the cab floor.

This cylinder uses the standard "D"–type sliding valve, a design that works well enough for lower-pressure engines working in the 150psi and below range, but subject to rapid wear in higher-pressure systems.

Chapter 3

4-4-0 American

Although American railroads began operation with imported British locomotives, experience quickly showed that local conditions required something different. American roadbeds were rough and full of sharp curves that frequently derailed the rigid wheel trucks of British models.

Henry Campbell, a Philadelphia resident and colleague of locomotive builder M. W. Baldwin, designed and patented a more flexible version of the import. Campbell used a pivoting four-wheel leading truck, introduced earlier on the Experiment, to support the front of the boiler, and used four drivers supporting the firebox. This arrangement helped align the driving wheels on curves and provided a stable three-point suspension that eliminated many of the problems with the earlier design. The twin drivers on each side offered support for a bigger boiler and a larger firebox, and the whole arrangement provided superior adhesion.

Campbell patented his design in February 1836 and promptly went to work on a new locomotive based on the design. The first example was finished in May 1837, a twelve-ton (10.8t) machine, much larger than most of its contemporaries.

The boiler, huge for its time, had a heating surface of 732 square feet (68 sq m)

Western Maryland Scenic's No. 734 **(opposite)** *is a veteran of the old Lake Superior & Ishpeming line, and now runs between Cumberland and Frostburg.* **ABOVE:** *Detail, 4-4-0 Jupiter at Promontory, Utah.*

and was designed to operate at 90psi. The massive cylinders, with a fourteen-inch (35.6cm) bore and seventeen-inch (43.2cm) stroke, drove fifty-four-inch (137.2cm) driving wheels. The new design provided more than 60 percent better traction than earlier locomotives and could pull a 450-ton (408t) train across level track at about 15mph (24kph).

This new 4-4-0 type quickly became accepted as the standard design for locomotives running all across North America. By 1850 the engine was the overwhelming choice for most applications, and factories were churning them out by the hundreds and thousands. By 1870, at the peak of this design's popularity, 85 percent of all American locomotives were of this type.

And the 4-4-0 has made its mark in the annals of history as well. Both of the locomotives that met at Promontory, Utah, in May 1869 for the driving of the Golden Spike, celebrating completion of the transcontinental railroad, were 4-4-0s.

However, the name "American" was not applied to the arrangement until 1870, after the design had been in production for thirty-five years and shortly before new and larger designs began to dominate the market.

EVOLUTION OF THE AMERICAN STANDARD LOCOMOTIVE

The 4-4-0 American Standard displaced the 4-2-0 about 1840 and dominated the locomotive industry for the next forty years. These machines typically weighed about ninety thousand pounds (40,860kg), operated at around 100psi, were nearly fifty-five-feet (16.8m) long, and could generate around seven thousand pounds (3,180kg) of tractive effort. Although capable of reaching speeds of 60mph (97kph), these locomotives usually averaged about only 25mph (40kph).

The first 4-4-0s were tiny things, about twelve or fifteen tons (11–13.5t). They lacked cabs and could generate only enough steam to run at about 15 mph (24kph). But their basic pattern was obviously sound and the design lasted for nearly one hundred years of production.

JUPITER

Most books on locomotives claim that the last American steamer was built back in the late 1950s, and they say that the last 4-4-0 American Standard was manufactured in 1928. Neither of those assertions is really correct.

Two complete and authentic steam locomotives were built in the late 1970s, and both were American Standards. The customer was the National Park Service, which purchased both engines for display and operation at the new Golden Spike National Historic Site at Promontory, Utah, where the transcontinental railroad was joined in May 1869.

Sierra Railroad's No. 8 has been another frequent bit player in Hollywood features. Out behind the roundhouse are several big balloon smokestacks, used to give the old girl an antique appearance.

Bob Dowty Steaming Up *Jupiter* and No. 119

Bob Dowty is the senior engineer at the Golden Spike National Historic Site. Here, he explains how he fires up Jupiter *and No. 119 or a day's operation.*

There is a lot of preparation to steaming up. Bob Dowty starts the task each day on No. 119, starting with a long process of preparation. A careful inspection of the fire box and water level is followed by clean-up of the ashes from the previous days fire. Then, it's time to start the fire, and repeat the process on *Jupiter*. Here is Dowty's explanation of what it takes to get both engines going:

With Number 119, which burns coal, it takes about ten minutes to get all the ash and cinders off the grate. Then we spread a thin layer of coal across the grate, pile some kindling on top, then splash some diesel fuel on the wood. A small blower adds some draft and we toss in a match. The fire will begin to burn.

As soon as 119's fire is started, we go to work on *Jupiter*. Since she's a wood-burner, there is virtually no ash on the grates. Wood disappears almost completely during the burning process, unlike coal. We fill the firebox about half full of wood, put some diesel fuel on a piece of cotton waste, and light the fire.

It takes about four hours to get *Jupiter* fully steamed up if she is completely cold, an hour and a half if she's still warm from the previous day.

During the summer months, the boilers will hold some heat and pressure overnight. It isn't unusual for 119 to still have forty psi in the morning. That makes steaming up much faster.

Her boiler contains about 820 gallons [3,104l] of water with the level at half a glass, the normal operating quantity. The boiler will actually hold nine hundred gallons [3,407l], but that's way too much for operation. That's not a lot for a

This glittering creature is actually a modern steam locomotive, built in the 1970s to be an almost perfect copy of Jupiter, one of the two locomotives that met on this spot in 1869 to join the transcontinental railroad.

steam engine, and four hours is not a long time to get pressure up.

While both engines are getting up steam, we "oil around," as old-time engineers used to say. We take our long oil cans and go around to all the oil cups where the locomotives need lubrication. We wipe down anyplace where dirt or oil has accumulated.

The water level in the tenders is checked; they are filled every day, even though we can go three days with a full one. But the only brakes we have on the engine are actually on the tender; the weight of the water is important for adhesion. We also monitor the chemicals in the water. An anti-foaming compound and corrosion-resistant chemicals are used to keep the boiler clean.

Jupiter and 119 are both very simple to operate, compared to later models. We don't have automatic air brakes, only engine brakes on the tender. You have to be a bit cautious about where you go and when you decide to apply the brakes because if you're not careful, you can lock those brakes up and skid into a crash.

There is no greater thrill than to take a cold, dead, old steam locomotive (and there is nothing deader than a dead steam locomotive) and put water in it, build a fire in its firebox—to smell the coal smoke, feel the heat, listen to the boiler water simmering— and when it is finally steamed up, to blow the whistle, open the throttle, and to make it come to life and move.

At the time that the specifications for these locomotives were being written, someone on the design committee attempted to simulate a locomotive using a fiberglass shell around diesel or electric power sources. Fortunately, the final contract went to a bidder who promised to build faithful reproductions of the *Jupiter* and the 119, the two original locomotives that met at Promontory.

Constructed using modern steel and fabrication techniques, both locomotives were built to be much safer and more durable than the originals; otherwise, they are virtually identical. The contractor was O'Connor Engineering in Costa Mesa, California.

Bob Dowty worked on both machines. He is now the Master Mechanic at Promontory, and here's what he has to say about them:

We started on these locomotives in August 1977 and delivered them April 30, 1979. The cost was $750,000 each, and that helped make Jupiter as authentic as modern technology would allow, while still considering visitor safety and operating efficiency. We used state-of-the-art machining and metallurgy in its construction and the boiler was built to American Society of Mechanical Engineers (ASME) standards. Much to the chagrin of many rail fans, that means no rivets—the boiler is welded. But otherwise the boilers are nearly identical to the original. We built two nineteenth-century locomotives to twentieth-century standards.

Chad O'Connor wasn't the low bidder—he bid high, based on the quality of work he thought the project deserved. The committee liked his presentation and he got the job. He and Maury Hauser and others went to work on the engineering drawings. Maury did all the valve-gear layout, a critical part of a steam locomotive.

By the end of the nineteenth century, 4-4-0 American Standard locomotives were bigger, stronger, and faster than their forebears of half a century before. Below, a train crew pauses for a group portrait.

FOLLOWING PAGES: The Virginia & Truckee railroad served the silver mining area around Carson City, Nevada. This venerable 4-4-0 is fitted with a huge snowplow designed to cope with the twenty-foot (6m) drifts common on the line.

VIRGINIA & TRUCKEE.
18

VIRGINIA & TRUCKEE
1015

New York Central No. 999	
Length overall, including tender	57 feet, 10 inches (17.6m)
Weight, in working order	204,000 pounds (92,616kg)
Boiler pressure	190psi
Drivers	86 inches (218.5cm)
Maximum tractive effort	16,280 pounds (7,391kg)
Grate area	32 square feet (3 sq m)
Fuel type and capacity	Coal, 14,140 pounds (6,420kg)
Heated surface area	1,930 square feet (179.5 sq m)
Cylinder bore x stroke	19 inches by 24 inches (48.3x61cm)

O'Connor did a lot of the big stuff, and some of it was very big, twenty feet [6m] long in some cases!

An engineer from 1869 could climb into the cab of *Jupiter* or 119 and recognize everything except the air brakes, and that wouldn't take him long to figure out.

The driving wheels and truck wheels are cast in modern manganese steel, not the brittle cast iron of the original. The boilers are made of modern steel. We used modern machineing techniques . . . A computerized automatic flame-cutting machine followed the blue-print, leaving a single, strong homogenous frame far stronger than the fabricated 1868 original.

AMERICAN-CLASS LOCOMOTIVES ON DISPLAY

Perhaps the prettiest operational American-class 4-4-0 locomotives can be found at Promontory, Utah. There at Golden Spike National Historic Site, the National Park Service displays and operates recreations of the two original locomotives that met at the completion of the transcontinental railroad in 1869: *Jupiter* and Union Pacific's No. 119.

Number 999, the New York Central locomotive that made that 112-mph (180kph) run way back in 1883, still survives and is on display at the Chicago Museum of Science and Industry.

*American railroads helped revolutionize logistics during the Civil War, moving troops, supplies, artillery, horses, and equipment with speed previously undreamed of. Much of that movement was accomplished with 4-4-0 locomotives like this one (**opposite**).*

A very small 4-4-0 with a very big trailing load of redwood logs.

YARD
LIMIT
1385
LACKAWANNA
1385

4-6-0 Ten-Wheeler

Ten-wheelers never acquired the glory of the American Standard, and were never christened with a charming nickname. Even so, there were hordes of them running the rails in the late nineteenth and early twentieth centuries. They were workhorse engines, reliable performers, pulling freights and passenger consists everywhere.

For many years, the 4-6-0 was the most adaptable locomotive on American rails, suitable for fast passenger service or slow, economical freight operations. It was the state of the art, for a while, and despite the lack of a catchy nickname, ten wheelers caught the American spot light for about twenty years. Casey Jones was driving a ten wheeler, Illinois Central 382, when he met his legendary death in April, 1900—and three other trainmen would die in that same locomotive in later years, after it was rebuilt.

The great virtue of the design, at that time, was that it offered better adhesion and power than the popular the 4-4-0 American Standard, with the same wheel loading. One typical application for the 4-6-0 during the last years of the ninteenth century was high-speed passenger service. These locomotives, with huge drivers, were frequently seen at the head of a consist of five or six passenger cars, roaring along the mainline at about seventy miles (112.6km) per hour.

Chicago & Northwestern's No. 1385 (left) chuffs through the woods outside North Freedom, Wisconsin. The ten-wheeler never got much glory, but late in the nineteenth century, it was seen everywhere, doing everything.

They lasted into the 1940s in great numbers, but not on the mainline. You could see them puttering along the uneven backwoods roadbeds of the South and more remote regions of the West. Few of them had the flash and dash of the bigger, faster locomotives that came later, but they were survivors—and many still survive today.

CHESAPEAKE: THE FIRST TEN-WHEELER

The ten-wheeler originated in 1847 as a new locomotive for the Philadelphia & Reading Railroad. Built by the Norris shops, it was named the *Chesapeake*. It was a muscular and oversized machine for its time, weighing 44,070 pounds (20,008kg), with its tender holding two cords of wood and two thousand gallons (7,570l) of water. Cylinders were 14.5 inches (36.8cm) by twenty-two inches (56cm) and were powered by a boiler with 133 tubes, each two inches (5cm) in diameter and twelve feet (3.7m) long.

Chesapeake was designed to pull one hundred loaded coal cars, a trailing load weighing 710 tons (644t), and did everything expected of her. She was fired for the first time on March 15, 1847, and delivered two days later. In May, her owners wrote Norris a complimentary note, stating, "The *Chesapeake* possesses to a greater extent than any other engine . . . the combined qualities of efficiency and ease to the rail and bridges."

One day after the *Chesapeake* was delivered, another builder delivered a similar ten-wheeler, the *New Hampshire*, to the Boston & Maine Railroad. A second ten-wheeler followed a few weeks later.

It took a few years for the ten-wheeler to really catch on, but this locomotive pattern became the second most popular engine during the latter half of the 1800s, second only to the 4-4-0 American Standard. The peak of ten-wheel success came around 1870, when it was shown to be the most powerful machine for freight work. Most locomotives, particularly the early examples, used small driving wheels suitable to slow speeds and heavy trailing loads. Then the early multipurpose engines lost favor to specialized locomotives designed to perform one particular chore with maximum efficiency. The ten-wheeler faded quickly from service on the main lines.

NEVADA NORTHERN'S No. 40

Many ten-wheelers continued to be built, used for backwoods and short line chores. Nevada Northern's 1910 Baldwin No. 40 is one, a sturdy engine whose former career included hauling ore cars to the Kennicott Copper smelter nearby.

No. 40 was built specifically for Nevada Northern and was intended for passenger use on the long, lonesome line between East Ely and the Southern Pacific

By the turn of the century, locomotive instrumentation **(preceding page)** *had developed to a high level of precision and reliability.*
RIGHT: *The Sierra Railroad is now operated by the California State Railroad museum. Even so, it remains one of the more authentic operations. Its old roundhouse is full of a century's accumulation of grease, grime, exotic tools, and working locomotives.*

Detail, valve gear, Sierra
Railroad No. 28.

Early on a winter morning, Sierra Railroad's oil-burning No. 28's (above) steam gauge is finally up to working pressure.

Belfast & Moosehead Lake's No. 1149 (right) seems to have taken a wrong switch somewhere along the line—she's an ex-Swedish State Railways locomotive now roaming the rails near Unity, Maine.

Milwaukee Road's beautiful No. 261 rests at Galesburg, Illinois.

Hot to trot, Osceola &
St. Croix Valley Railway's
No. 328 simmers while getting up steam. This well-
preserved ten-wheeler was
built by ALCO in 1907, and
originally worked for the
Northern Pacific.

Steam is allowed to vent through the cylinder and associated plumbing, warming the cold steel and iron before getting under way.

main line more than one hundred miles (161km) to the north at Cobra. And that's exactly what the locomotive's job was for the next thirty years.

A massive chunk of scrap iron the size of a locomotive was tempting during World War II, and No. 40 was scheduled to be cut up. The chief mechanical officer and several other workers decided that the old locomotive was too good for scrap, so they hatched a plan to prevent her from going to the cutting torches. Whenever one of the senior officers or supervisors came

around, they made sure No. 40 was safely hidden—hard to do with a massive locomotive, but they succeeded and she survived. After the war, when it was safe for the locomotive to reappear, No. 40 was used occasionally for special passenger runs and other duties until 1983. Then, very suddenly, Nevada Northern shut down. It closed its doors one day and sent everybody home. Almost all the staff expected the line to reopen any day—but weeks turned to months, months to years, and the whole railroad collected dust.

When the state of Nevada finally acquired the line in the early 1990s, state historian Sean Pitts, walked into a railroading time capsule. No. 40 was virtually ready to fire up and was put back into revenue service after a little work on the leaky tender. She runs most weekends during the spring, summer, and autumn, on a route around town and out into the desert. You can rent No. 40 for a couple of hours of instruction; the current cost is $550 if you want to go out on the main line, $350 if you stay in the yard.

This sturdy ten-wheeler is an ex–Chicago & Northwestern locomotive now in tourist service, pausing for water before a day's service.

BALDWIN LOCOMOTIVE WORKS
2
PHILADELPHIA.U.S.A.

CHAPTER 5

2-8-2 Mikado

Toward the end of the nineteenth century, nations around the world were building rail systems, often buying imported locomotives for their new railroads. Japan was a typical customer for imported engines in 1893. Using the standard three-foot, six-inch (106.5cm) track gauge, it too ordered its new engines from Baldwin.

The Japanese requested locomotives with two leading truck wheels, eight drivers, and two trailing wheels supporting an enlarged firebox. Although the Japanese engines were not the first, they were the first successful examples of the type. In honor of the purchaser and a Gilbert and Sullivan opera of a few years earlier, the new breed was christened Mikado.

Baldwin built a few more Mikado engines during the next few years, but they took a while to catch on. The first American company to buy was the Bismarck, Washburn & Great Falls Railroad, which bought just one, in 1902. Santa Fe ordered fifteen the same year, but it was the Northern Pacific that really took a shine to the "Mike," requisitioning 160 of them during the next five years, all from Brooks Locomotive Works.

Then, around the time of World War I, the Mike became everybody's favorite freight locomotive. The configuration typically used smallish drivers, about sixty

Saginaw Timber No. 2 (left) is a small example of a 2-8-2 Mikado, a veteran of the lumber boom during the early part of the twentieth century. ABOVE: Detail, Valley Railroad No. 40.

inches (152.5cm) in diameter, designed to deliver lots of power at low speed, with a good-sized firebox that could generate sufficient steam for heavy loads.

VALLEY RAILROAD NO. 40

Tucked away in one of the most unspoiled places in North America is a little railroad called the Valley Railroad. There, you can find a small, old, perfectly functional Mikado. No. 40 was built in August 1920 by ALCO at its Brooks Locomotive Works in Dunkirk, New York. Many of the locomotives coming out of the Brooks Works back then were headed west, and No. 40 was no exception. Her original buyer was the Oregon Lumber Company, and she was destined to haul timber.

No. 40 is a good example of a typical logging and short line locomotive of the time. It's a small, muscular engine designed for go rather than for show. All those drivers helped make the little Mike very muscular indeed.

"Number 40 is pretty typical of small logging 2-8-2 locomotives of the time," according to Dave Conrad, chief mechanical officer for Valley Railroad. "It has 48-inch [122cm] driving wheels, the cylinders are 20 inches by 28 inches [51x71cm], designed for 180 psi operation when it was new. We've cut that back to 175 psi. Tractive effort for the locomotive is about 35,000 pounds [15,890kg]."

The little No. 40 worked in the Oregon woods until the timber was cut down, then it was sold to the Minarets & Western Railroad in California. That assignment lasted for six years, until the company went out of business. No. 40 was turned over to Southern Pacific Railroad as compensation for debts owed. SP didn't need it, so No. 40 was sold again, this time to a used-locomotive dealer, Birmingham Rail & Locomotive Company, which in turn sold it to the Aberdeen & Rockfish Railroad in North Carolina. That was in the 1930s.

Aberdeen & Rockfish kept No. 40 in heat for the next two decades, until the middle 1950s. Then, instead of being scrapped like so many of her contemporaries, No. 40 sat in a shed for another twenty years.

She was discovered by some folks from the Valley Railroad and purchased, complete with lots of tools and spare parts, in 1977. No. 40 was moved up to Essex, Connecticut, fired up, and put back to work. This time her job was hauling tourists along the lovely Connecticut River. She ran from 1977 to 1985, when a driving wheel tire broke and the engine was taken out of service once again. Dave Conrad notes:

When I came to work here in 1986, I evaluated the locomotives lying derelict around the property, trying to decide which one to work on first. Number 40 was our choice. We went to work on it in 1988.

Valley Railroad's Mikado (left) is a long way from the Oregon woods where she worked early in the century, but her new home in Connecticut is a happy one.

Saginaw Timber No. 2 (above) is a 1912 Baldwin currently performing at the Mid-Continent Railway Museum, near North Freedom, Wisconsin.

*Boone & Scenic's route traverses the Des Moines River Valley, some of Iowa's most attractive terrain (**left**), complete with a high bridge for the locomotive to pose upon.* **BELOW:** *Specifications for Boone & Scenic's Chinese Mikado.* **OPPOSITE:** *Detail, Mikado locomotive.*

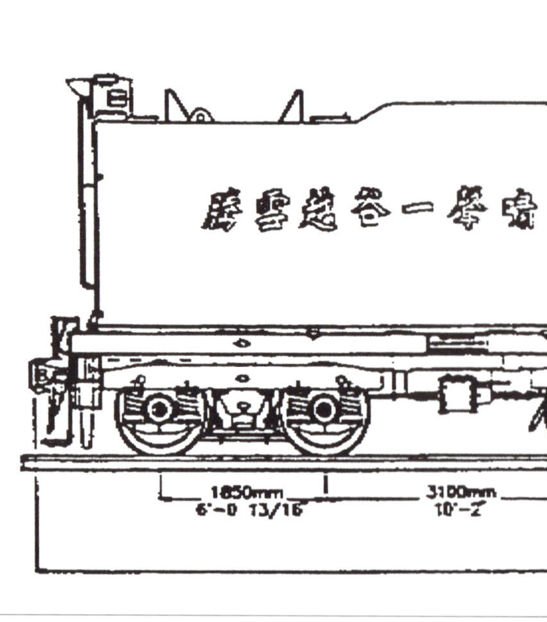

As is typical with locomotive restorations, the project snowballed. We started to replace just some driving wheel tires and make some general repairs, then put it back in service. But once we got the drivers off, we found two cracked axles and another axle that was undersize. So we decided that since we were already committed to big money on the project, we might as well do all the repairs at the same time.

Number 40 received all new driving axles, all new tires, one complete new driving wheel. The crank pins were all renewed. Since we didn't have the large press required to refit them, we made the parts and then shrunk them in liquid nitrogen. Then we slipped them in their holes; when the pins warmed back up they were there to stay!

All the bearings were replaced, the running gear overhauled, cylinders and pistons all reworked. Then we replaced the 'shoes' and 'wedges,' consumable parts used

between the locomotive frame and the driving box. Proper alignment of these parts is essential to ensure the locomotive rides down the track properly, without wearing out the driving wheels or derailing. Part of the shoe and wedge job involves stringing piano wire through the bore of the cylinder and extending it past the back of the frame. By pulling the wire tight, you have a reference line that can be used to 'prove' the alignment of the frame. This work assured the driving axles were all parallel to each other and perpendicular to the bore of the cylinders.

The tender was overhauled, the locomotive re-tubed, all the accessories like the air compressor, dynamo, and power reverse reworked. Then in December of 1992 the job was done and it was put back in service. Number 40 has been our mainstay ever since. We put about 7,000 miles [11,200km] on it each year.

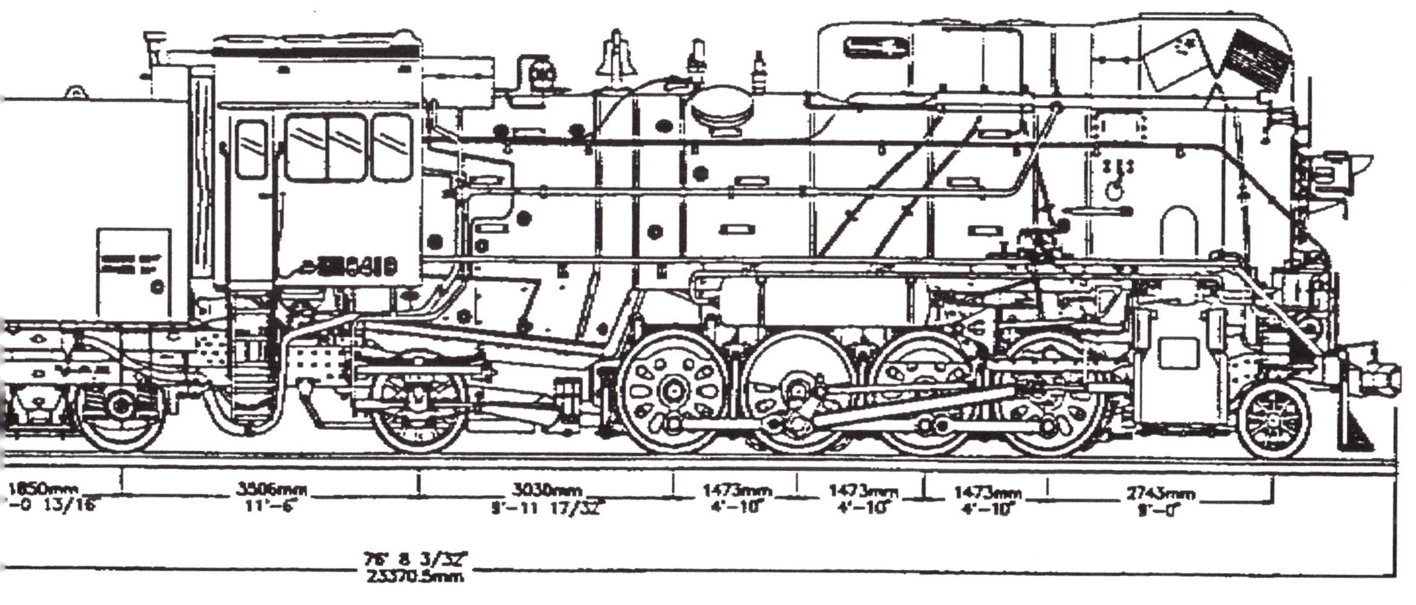

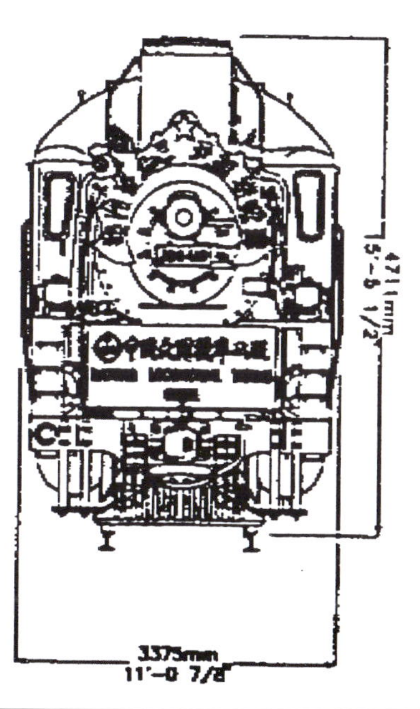

Your Hand on the Throttle

Amateurs can learn the basics of steam locomotive operations from experienced engineers.

Valley Railroad offers a short course in locomotive operation. You can actually take control of No. 700 for an hour under the guidance of a qualified engineer. It isn't cheap, at about $300 per hour, but that's about the same price charged by other groups offering the same kind of instruction. It has been a highly popular program for Valley Railroad, and sessions are typically booked weeks in advance.

"People come away from the sessions raving about the experience. It's a wonderful experience when a lifelong dream is realized," Dave Conrad says, "and people seem to think that, considering how special the opportunity is, the cost is reasonable."

The whole package at Valley Railroad includes a book on steam technology and locomotive operation, an hour-long classroom session on safety and the technology of the locomotive, then a session of actual operation of the locomotive.

Wannabe-engineers can take control of the locomotives of yesteryear at many historic railroad sites across North America.

JS8419

A Chinese Mike

We're all so accustomed to thinking of steam locomotives as ancient, worn-out artifacts that visitors to Iowa's Boone & Scenic Railroad are often shocked to discover a nearly new steam engine simmering purposefully at the head of a procession of passenger cars.

The locomotive is an import from China that was built in 1989. It is a large JS-class Mikado numbered 8419. Although they are slowly converting to diesel and electric power, the Chinese are still using steam locomotives to transport goods across their vast nation today. No. 8419 was the final JS-class engine built by the Datong Company and is one of three purchased for use in the United States.

Boone & Scenic came up with $350,000 for the Mike; it cost $100,000 just for shipping to Los Angeles. Private sources and money from the Iowa Development Commission Fund made the deal. Even though the locomotive was dropped and slightly damaged during unloading, it was soon in operation in central Iowa.

Despite its foreign origins, the Chinese Mike is right at home on American rails. She was built for 4-foot, 8½-inch (143.5cm) gauge, the standard in China as well as most of North America. Many of her accessories are near duplicates of common equivalents here. The air compressor is an apparent copy of a Westinghouse model, for instance, and the couplers are identical to and compatible with those used in the United States

"One common question we get from people is, 'What did you have to do to get it ready to run on American tracks?' " notes Ed Truslow, General Manager of Boone & Scenic. "The answer is, 'virtually nothing!' The standard track gauge in China is the same as in the United States and most of the rest of the world. The couplers work the same way as standard American couplers and we could hook it up directly to our American cars. The brakes are the same 6T standard used on other locomotives. The biggest difference is that the engineer sits on the left side of the cab, in English fashion, rather than on the right as do American engineers. The similarities far outweigh the differences you might naturally expect in a Chinese copy of an American design. The air pump looks like a Westinghouse compressor, injectors look like standard injectors, and the throttle, brake stand, lubricators, and many other components look exactly like those found on standard American steam locomotives."

"It is quite a historic locomotive," Truslow reports. "It is the only JS-class locomotive outside China, and quite possibly the last production locomotive built in the world."

Boone & Scenic operates its Chinese Mike three times a day on weekends and holidays, from Memorial Day through the last weekend in October. The trip is a beautiful 20-mile (32km) expedition through the Des Moines River Valley, across a 150-foot (46m) bridge, and it traverses some long grades. The grades give the engine a real chance to show its stuff, but even with all nine passenger cars packed to the gills, the big Mikado hardly feels the load.

All locomotive operations are performed by volunteers who've completed a long and exacting training process. But just about anyone can take the controls of the big Mike—like other such steam operators, Boone & Scenic will let you shovel coal and drive the locomotive for a $350 fee.

Engine crews show up at 7:30 A.M. on days when the steamer is in operation, build the fire, get the steam pressure up, and perform routine maintenance. Once there's pressure, they blow down the engine, top off water and coal, and are ready for the first run at 11:00 A.M. They are back for their second run at 1:30 P.M., and the last trip at 4:00 P.M. With luck, the tired and grimy volunteers have the Mike tied up, safe and sound, at about 6:30 P.M., and can go home to clean up. That comes close to the twelve-hour limit for train crews imposed by the Federal Railroad Administration.

"I think our scenery is some of the most gorgeous of any scenic railway in America, possibly excluding some of the Colorado lines," Ed says. "We go down into the Des Moines River Valley, and during the fall, when all the trees turn color, we get a lot of tourists.

"The locomotive could easily handle two or three times the load we put on it. Even in the fall when we have our heaviest trains, it scarcely notices the load. Coming back up out of the Des Moines River Valley we have a nice, four-mile-long [6.5km] 1.5 percent grade that gives it a little workout. You set the throttle, set the Johnson bar, and cruise up the hill with the locomotive chugging away."

Western Maryland Scenic's No. 734 (far left), ready for another run from Cumberland, Maryland.
LEFT: *Saginaw Timber's No. 2 maneuver's under the watchful eye of her conductor.*

2472
P-8
SP 110300 LBS I.T

Chapter 6

4-6-2 Pacific Locomotive

Pacific locomotives aren't the biggest, the most powerful, or the most elegant machines to have steamed the rails, but they are survivors. Great numbers are still in existence and still in action around the United States and Canada. Their popularity is due to their size and adaptability.

Introduced at the turn of the twentieth century, the midsize Pacific was available in several models, from a smallish logging engine to a large main line passenger locomotive. The Pacific was so popular around the world that an orchestral work was written in its honor—Symphonic Movement Number 1, "Pacific 231," by Arthur Honneger, followed by an experimental 1948 film of the same name by French cinematographer Jean Mitry.

The true parentage of the first Pacific is in doubt. A locomotive with the 4-6-2 wheel arrangement was assembled by the Vulcan Iron Works of Wilkes-Barre, Pennsylvania, for the Lehigh Valley Railroad back in 1886. It was a double camel-back engine laid out by George Strong, but the design deleted the two trailing wheels early in life. George Drury reports that similar designs soon appeared—one built by the Schenectady Locomotive Works in 1887, several others by other builders in 1893. However, none

Southern Pacific's wonderful Pacific No. 2472 (left) hauled commuter trains from 1921 until 1957, then spent years as a rusting display in a park. Now, fully restored, she returns to Santa Clara depot during an excursion run.
ABOVE: *Detail, SP No. 2472.*

seems to have worked well and all were soon modified back into ten-wheelers.

Many historians generally accept a Baldwin engine built in 1901 as the ancestor of the 4-6-2 Pacific tribe. Destined for export to New Zealand, the design was highly successful—bigger, with more power, speed, and traction than the Atlantic or Mogul.

The first Pacific for North American use was delivered in 1902 from the Brooks Locomotive Works shops in Dunkirk, New York, to the Missouri Pacific and the St. Louis Iron Mountain & Southern Railroads.

That same year, the Chesapeake & Ohio introduced its own version, known as the F15 4-6-2 Pacific class. All of these Pacifics combined exceptional speed and power, and Pacific locomotives promptly became the standard for fast main line passenger service. Many were used for such service until their owners converted to diesel. Overall, about seven thousand

Pacifics of all types were built before the last one was delivered in 1948.

This locomotive was a modification of the earlier 4-4-2 Atlantic, featuring an extra driver for better traction and a trailing axle for improved firebox support. On a classic Pacific, that trailing axle is well astern, directly under the firebox, and the firebox itself is noticeably larger than on earlier locomotives. That large furnace—a typical grate area of about fifty square feet (4.7 sq m) in early examples, with a heating surface of around three thousand square feet (729 sq m)—could produce a lot of steam! And with the extra axle, plus the added adhesive weight, the Pacific could really dig in its heels and push.

CHESAPEAKE & OHIO PACIFIC CLASS F15, 1902

A good early example of the breed is C&O's 1902 Pacific, built by ALCO and designated Class F15 by the C&O. At seventy-four feet (22.5m) long and weighing 408,000 pounds (185,232kg), it was a monster for its day. Grate area was seventy-four square feet (6.9 sq m), with a heated area of 2,938 square feet (273.2 sq m), a very large improvement over earlier boiler standards. Steam at 180 psi powered cylinders with 23.5-inch (60cm) bore and twenty-eight-inch (71cm) stroke. With driving wheels six feet (1.8m) tall, this variant generated 32,400 pounds (14,710kg) of tractive effort and proved to be quick and stable, just the thing for hauling heavy passenger cars at high speed. The tender provided fifteen tons (13.5t) of coal and nine thousand gallons (34,070l) of water.

PENNSYLVANIA RAILROAD PACIFIC CLASS K4, 1914

The Pennsylvania Railroad started buying Pacifics in 1907, well after other lines had them. The first came from ALCO, but in 1910 the Pennsylvania Railroad started

SP No. 2472 momentarily at rest, Burlingame, California. One of the problems for running this big locomotive is Southern Pacific's restrictions on when and where it can go. A mechanical problem could shut down the main line at tremendous cost to regular traffic.

You don't see this sort of thing very often—two muscular, beautiful steam locomotives (**above**) cruising the main line with a long consist of passenger cars. In this case, the locomotives are SP No. 4442, a Northern, and SP No. 2472, a Pacific-class locomotive.

Here's No. 2472 **(above)** during her prime, the late 1940s, hauling commuters home to stations between San Francisco and San Jose.

Reading Railroad's No. 111 **(right)** is a G-1a variant Pacific-class locomotive, built by Baldwin between 1916 and 1923. PAGE **76–77:** The "Bean Steam Special" with No. 2472 on the point skirts San Francisco Bay near the tiny community of Pinole.

building them in its own shops, a version first designated K2. Two hundred thirty-nine of these Pacifics were built, followed by K3s, with mechanical stokers, and then the K4 in 1914.

K4 Pacifics were now up to eighty-three feet (25m) long, with 553,000 pounds (251,062kg) of iron and steel and water, 4,040 square feet (375.7 sq m) of heating area, and operating at 205psi. Drivers on this model are eighty inches (203cm) in diameter, turned by cylinders twenty-seven inches (68.5cm) by twenty-eight (71cm) inches.

SOUTHERN PACIFIC'S NO. 2472—A SUCCESS STORY

Southern Pacific Railroad bought lots of 4-6-2 Pacific locomotives beginning in 1903. Most of these came from Baldwin, including fifteen built to SP's specification P-7 in 1921. These were workhorse machines, hauling main line passenger and freight consists early in their lives, then commuter passengers later.

No. 2472 was one of these. She hauled commuters between San Jose and San Francisco, California, in the years after World War II. Finally, after many miles and years of faithful service, SP retired the P-7s in favor of diesel in 1957. Most fell to the cutting torch, all except No. 2472 and a few others generously donated by the railroad to almost anybody who would take one and put it on display.

There was some vacant real estate in the San Mateo County, California, fairgrounds parking lot, and somebody decided No. 2472 could rest there. SP towed the derelict locomotive to a nearby siding, temporary track was constructed, and the old locomotive was put on display for the occasional amusement of visitors, a target for vandals, and something for children to climb upon. There No. 2472 rested until 1977.

X2475
2475

Southern Pacific No. 2472	
Length overall, including tender	89 feet, 7.75 inches (27.5m)
Weight, in working order	2,719,800 pounds (1,234,789kg)
Boiler pressure	210psi
Drivers	73 inches (185.5cm)
Maximum tractive effort	45,850 pounds (20,816kg)
Grate area	Not available
Tubes	193 2.25-inch (5.7cm) tubes
Tubes	40 5.5-inch (14cm) tubes
Fuel type	Oil
Heated surface area	3,352 square feet (311.7 sq m)
Cylinder bore x stroke	25 inches by 30 inches (63.5×76cm)

*S*P's No. 2475, a little *worse for wear, pauses momentarily during the 1950s.*

Mike Mangini, a rail fan and veteran of the 1976 American Freedom Train Project, noticed the decaying hulk. He asked if the county would permit the locomotive to be restored. The response was, "If that's what you want to do, go ahead—just get it out of the fairgrounds. It takes up parking spaces."

Mike and other volunteers formed a group and went to work on the locomotive. Since SP had prepared the old locomotive well when it had been taken out of service, it was in better shape than Mike and the other volunteers had anticipated.

But the boiler needed new tubes and superheaters, firebox welding, and stay bolt replacement. The frame and running gear also needed attention. So the locomotive was jacked up three feet (1m) and placed on heavy timbers while work proceeded on the axles and bearings.

SP locomotives are all notoriously grimy, and No. 2472 maintained the tradition, even in retirement. When the frame was being cleaned, a large crack was discovered. Welding facilities for making such repairs had disappeared when the old shops were demolished after the railroads converted to diesel. The crack appeared impossible to repair. Without a fix, No. 2472 couldn't be certified to run on the main line. "Never assume something is impossible until you find out for yourself," Mangini told his volunteers.

Modern halogen lamps were used to heat the area surrounding the crack to eighteen hundred degrees Fahrenheit (982°C), relieving the stress on the crack and permitting a deep weld to the fracture.

After thirteen years of effort, on February 10, 1990, old No. 2472 moved again, for the first time in thirty-one years. After more than another year of volunteer work, the big old Pacific boiler was fired up on April 26, 1991, working after more than thirty years of idleness. A week later, No. 2472 moved under its own power. A few days after that, on May 1, 1991, the old locomotive slowly moved out onto the Southern Pacific main line for a run to Railfair '91 in Sacramento, California.

No. 2472 is still running, fired up several times a year for excursions in the area. You can rent the locomotive and learn to run it yourself, or you can just watch it in action during one of its forays out of its engine house at Hunter's Point Naval Shipyard in San Francisco.

CHESAPEAKE & OHIO
614

CHAPTER 7

4-8-4 Northern Locomotive

If the 4-4-0 American Standard was the pet of the nineteenth century, then surely the 4-8-4 Northern type has been the favorite of the twentieth. The breed was highly sucessful during the late steam era and is still alive today. Not only are about a dozen of them still functional, but the Union Pacific's No. 844 has never been retired and still operates occasionally in revenue freight service.

Several versions of the Northern 4-8-4 pattern were designed and built at the same time, but the first to hit the rails was part of an order of twelve from the Northern Pacific Railroad to ALCO's Schenectady, New York, works. That first machine arrived in December 1926. The proud owners christened the type Northern Pacific, but everybody else just called it Northern. Well, almost everybody—the 4-8-4 is sometimes known in Canada as the Confederation type. Other railroads tried their own names on the new arrival: Dixie, Niagara, Pocono, Potomac, and Wyoming were all used. Northern is the only name that really stuck, though.

A typical Northern is an extremely powerful, efficient machine. It is heavier than a Boeing 747 and can carry one thousand passengers, three times the 747's capacity, or two thousand tons of freight (1,814t), thirty times that of the 747. With the massive drivers rotating at just 440 rpm, these giants move down the track at

Chesapeake & Ohio No. 614 (left), a superb example of the Northern class, poses for the camera outside Port Jervis, New York. ABOVE: *Detail, Milwaukee Road No. 261 Northern-class gauge.*

100 miles (161km) per hour. While the surviving Northerns aren't put at risk that way today, such speeds weren't uncommon back in the 1940s and '50s, when a hogger needed to make up time on sections where such speeds were authorized. And the great big Northerns could easily oblige, even with a trailing load of heavy freight or passenger cars.

More than one thousand Northerns were built between 1926 and that first order of twelve, and 1950, when the final example, Norfolk & Western's Number 613, rolled out of the shop.

The basic layout was just what North American railroads needed at the time. The Northern had enough power and endurance for pulling long trailing loads at high speeds, thanks to the four-wheel trailing truck, and good stability at speed, thanks to the leading two-axle truck. The design permitted a cavernous firebox, which was the key to the whole equation. The 4-8-4 became the new American stan-

C&O No. 614 is a 1948 product of the Lima Locomotive Works.

dard locomotive for "hotshot" passenger and freight consists on nearly every Class I railroad on the continent.

The typical Northern locomotive weighed about 425,000 pounds (192,950kg) alone, about 740,000 pounds (335,960kg) with its tender. The first batch built for the Northern Pacific Railroad were 105 feet (32m) long with a grate of 115 square feet (10.7 sq m), heated surface of 4,660 square feet (433.4 sq m), and cylinders twenty-eight inches (71cm) by thirty inches (76cm). Normal boiler pressure was a whopping 225psi, and when all that steam was vented into the cylinders, the first Northern used its eight big seventy-three-inch (185.5cm) drivers to generate 61,600 pounds (27,966kg) of tractive force. These engines all included superheaters, a kind of steam engine "afterburner" that added heat energy to the steam, improving performance substantially. They also had a booster added to the trailing truck, a small engine providing extra traction at low speeds—when starting a heavy train, for example, or going up a steep grade.

SOUTHERN PACIFIC GS-4 CLASS 4-8-4 NORTHERN

Southern Pacific's locomotives are noted as being generally grimy, unwashed creatures, laboring long and hard, often inside tunnels and snow sheds. But back in the 1940s and '50s, the big Northerns that were used to pull the Daylight between San Francisco and Los Angeles broke with tradition. These 4-8-4s gleamed in bright orange and red, a paint scheme applied to the whole train. Roaring down the West Coast through little farm communities and along the Pacific Ocean, the Daylight looked more like a rocket in horizontal flight. It was called the prettiest train in the world.

A big SP Northern is serviced during a halt. Maintenance requirements for steam locomotives had a lot to do with their demise; diesels require far less attention.

Head end view of No. 4449 **(below)** in its glittering, restored condition, during a visit to Redding, California.

No. 4449 crosses the Sacramento River Canyon **(right)** near Lakehead, California.

PNWC 4219
SOUTHERN PACIFIC
4449
Daylight

SP locomotive No. 4449 was one of these, part of a group of twenty-eight purchased from the Lima Locomotive Works in 1941 and 1942. Southern Pacific designated these as GS-4s, and they were a tremendous success.

Each weighed 883,000 pounds (400,882kg), burned oil instead of coal, operated at 300psi, and used monster driving wheels eighty inches (203cm) in diameter. Tractive effort was a tremendous 71,173 pounds (32,313kg), enough to haul

the Daylight easily across some steep grades and twisting roadbed. The Daylight averaged about 50mph (80kph) for the 470-mile (756km) run along the coast; not bad considering the steep grades near San Luis Obispo and the weight of the twelve trailing cars.

Partly because of the demanding route, No. 4449 and her sisters had added technical innovations that were missing from most of their contemporaries. One of these was electro-pneumatic (EP) braking,

Early in its second career, No. 4449 (above) toured the nation during the Bicentennial celebration, powering the American Freedom Train. Here she is at Forest, Mississippi.

C&O No. 614 (opposite) near Tuxedo, New York.

a technology in extensive use today but rare in the 1940s. Back then, brakes were applied by a reduction of air pressure only within the brake line. On a long train, the delay before full application could be several seconds. The EP system speeded up the process, a major safety enhancement.

The GS series used other leading-edge technologies for that day—three turbogenerators, a fuel economy indicator for the engineer, and a device inside the boiler to help suppress foaming. These locomotives also carried two thousand pounds (908kg) of sand, a lot more than flatland locomotives and yet another distinguishing feature.

Overall, these GS Northerns were basically conventional for their time. Other, bigger locomotives would use double-expansion cylinders, articulated frames, and even turbine engines. The Northerns were the epitome of the classic main line fast locomotive—and still are today.

SP&S No. 700

One of the three largest operational steam locomotives today is the Spokane, Portland & Seattle Railroad No. 700. This locomotive is the third largest operational steamer in North America and the second most powerful; only the Union Pacific's giant, articulated Challenger can outpull it.

SP&S No. 700 came from Baldwin in 1938, part of a group of three intended for fast passenger and freight service between Spokane and Vancouver, Washington. All three normally pulled night trains between the two cities until just after World War II, when the SP&S and its parent company, the Great Northern, started converting their fleet to diesel power.

No. 700 pulled secondary passenger trains for another few years and then was demoted to freight work in the early 1950s. While the rest of the steam fleet went

Union Pacific No. 844	
Length overall, including tender	114 feet (35m)
Weight, in working order	907,890 pounds (412,182kg)
Boiler pressure	300psi
Drivers	80 inches (203cm)
Maximum tractive effort	63,800 pounds (28,965kg)
Grate area	Removed; oil burner
Tubes	198 2.25-inch (5.7cm) tubes
Fuel type and capacity	Oil, #5 grade, 6,000 gallons (22,712l)
Heated surface area	
Evaporating surfaces	4,224 square feet (392.8 sq m)
Superheating surface	1,440 square feet (133.9 sq m)
Cylinder bore x stroke	25 inches by 32 inches (63.5x81cm)

Sadly, this lovely streamlined Northern from the Grand Trunk Western Railway (left) didn't survive the purges at the beginning of the diesel era.

quietly to the cutting torch, No. 700 was cleaned and painted for one last run. They called it Farewell to Steam, and hundreds of people signed up for the last trip, from Portland, Oregon, to Wishram, Washington.

Instead of going to the scrap heap, No. 700 went to a Portland city park for static display in 1958. It sat there for nearly twenty years before a kid with a passion for steam, fifteen-year-old Chris McLarney, went to work on the locomotive. After a couple of years, Chris recruited some

helpers and founded an organization called the Portland Railroad Preservation Association. Fifteen years after Chris started tinkering, No. 700 came back to life in 1990 and has been running the rails along the Columbia River and the Northwest ever since.

This healthy Northern is about seventy feet (21.5m) long exclusive of tender and seventeen feet (5m) tall at the stack, with drivers seventy-seven inches (195.5cm) in diameter. She burns oil, not coal.

Northern Class Steaming Survivors

Southern Pacific No. 4449

Union Pacific No. 844

Norfolk Western No. 611

Santa Fe No. 3751

Spokane, Portland & Seattle No. 700

Chesapeake & Ohio No. 614

Milwaukee Road No. 261

Getting Started on Milwaukee Road No. 261

Engineer Steve Sandberg shares his experiences operating one of the most active steam locomotives around.

One of the more active large steam locomotives running the rails in North America is North Star Rail's No. 261, an ex-Milwaukee Road Northern often piloted by Steve Sandberg. North Star uses the big Northern for fairly frequent excursions in the upper Midwest.

No. 261 was built by ALCO's Schenectady, New York, works for Milwaukee Road in 1944, a dual-service Northern type of locomotive expected to work both fast passenger and freight assignments. Her seventy-four-inch (188cm) drivers are a bit larger than those strictly freight Northerns use. No. 261 is a pretty modern steam locomotive, one of the last built, with some of the best refinements, like roller bearings. Milwaukee Road designated this hybrid design as its S3 class. Here are Steve's thoughts on the 261.

Number 261 was designed to carry twenty-five tons [22.5t] of coal; she has been modified to carry thirty tons [27t], enough for 325 miles [523km] of main line travel with a typical passenger consist on Midwestern prairie roadbed. The tender's water tank is good for only about 250 miles [402km]. Fifty years ago, refueling wasn't a problem since coaling towers and water tanks were stationed

along every line at frequent intervals. They are all gone now, and coal comes from a truck, water from a hydrant.

Number 261 is a very smooth-riding locomotive. It was sprung very well and rides like a Cadillac. It's a good locomotive, very well suited for today's main line railroads. It

has a very good feed water injector system, and it has full roller bearings. Roller bearing engines were designed to hook onto a long passenger or freight train and pull it from Chicago to Los Angeles without relief. Friction-bearing engines typically were not supposed to do that. Today most of the

Northern-type locomotives still in service are roller-bearing locomotives.

One important consideration for the engineer of a passenger train is to maintain slack on the couplers between cars when starting or stopping. You keep the train stretched out with a technique called "power braking." As you come into a station, you apply the train brakes first, to keep the individual cars stretched out, so there is no slack. You do the same thing when starting. Keep the train line brake applied as you apply power to the engine.

Okay, so you're sitting on the right side of the cab, with four critical controls in front of you: the Johnson bar or power reverse lever, the throttle, the engine brake, and the train line air brake. The power reverse control sets the valve that admits steam to the 261's cylinders. It can apply full pressure for the whole piston stroke, or just a short portion. On older engines with Johnson bars, this control is entirely manual and takes plenty of brawn to operate. Valve control on a 261 is air-actuated and much easier to operate. Take the power reverse lever and move it to the full forward position.

Next, open the cylinder cocks. A lever opens these drains on the bottom of the cylinders. A lot of water will have condensed inside the cylinders while 261 has been sitting idle. Unless this water is drained, hydraulic pressure will rip the cylinder heads right off as the throttle is opened. Standard procedure for starting any steam locomotive is to open these drains while starting.

Make sure the train brake is still set, then crack the throttle just a little bit. Steam starts flowing to the cylinders, much of its pressure blasting out the cylinder cocks, ejecting any liquid water. Now reach down to the sander control and apply some sand for traction.

Okay, now you're leaving the station and it's time to close the cylinder cocks and maybe apply some more sand. Your train is nicely stretched out and you've moved ahead five or ten feet [1.5–3m].

Now is the time to really lay into that throttle and open it up about 30 to 50 percent of its travel. Your cylinder pressure gauge will now indicate about 150 psi. A lot of the 275 psi boiler pressure is being fed to the cylinders and the engine really starts to work.

The fireman will be watching you. Now, with the engine rapidly draining the boiler of its steam, he turns on the stoker to keep the pressure up. He also watches the water level to make sure it doesn't fall too far.

The power reverse control is wide open, full forward, but now that the train is moving at about ten miles [16km] per hour, you can pull it back about one inch or so. This cuts off some of the steam feeding to the cylinders, making them more efficient. With the valve wide open, the locomotive was giving you all the power available. As you begin to close this control, it will start to give you speed instead.

Now you're rolling along at about twelve or fourteen miles [19–22.5km] per hour and you can close the valve a little more. The engine will work a little lighter. Apply some more sand and now open the throttle to feed full boiler pressure to the cylinders. If the fireman has done his job and kept it up at 275 psi, you can really pick up speed. If he has allowed it to drop, your speed will be limited. It is very hard to get that pressure back once it has been lost.

As you lay into it, apply more sand. If the locomotive starts to lose traction, you will feel it on the 261 because it will begin to vibrate a bit just before the wheels start to spin. A good engineer will catch that and back off the throttle right away and apply sand to keep adhesion between wheel and rail. If the wheels break traction, the speedometer will suddenly take off, a sure indication that you've lost your grip on the rails. If you don't regain traction, the engine will run away and destroy itself, so this is something to carefully avoid.

But if the engine is sticking to the rail and the throttle is wide open, you'll be accelerating through thirty, forty, and fifty miles [48–80km] per hour. You'll hear the powerful bark of the full-pressure steam blasting out through the cylinder exhausts at 250 psi; it sounds wonderfully powerful but actually indicates that you're wasting expensive steam. Now is the time to come back on the power reverse control, cutting off some of that steam. The engine doesn't slow down, but the amount of steam and coal and water consumed starts to drop dramatically. Now you're cruising!

Chapter 8

The Challenger and Other Monsters

Back in the 1920s and '30s, steam locomotives started to outgrow their environ-ment. Remember that a steam locomotive's ability to pull a heavy load is directly related to its size and weight. As trailing loads increased, so did the need for big-ger and more powerful locomotives—huge engines with twenty wheels and lots of power.

Although many such monsters were built, almost none survive today except as static displays. Of the hundreds of cab-forward Mallets used by Southern Pacific, only one survives. It is housed at the California State Railroad Museum in Sacramento but doesn't steam.

CHALLENGER

Union Pacific resurrected a 4-6-6-4 Challenger over several years during the 1980s and restored it with volunteer labor from its employees. Today it sometimes runs across the UP system on special occa-sions. UP is unique among American rail-roads for keeping its steam heritage alive, much to the gratification of millions of rail fans. But it is a costly program and doesn't fit neatly into the usual justifications for steam operations. Steve Lee, manager of the Steam Operations program, explains:

The Challenger is thrilling to operate, but it is a lot of hot, hard, dirty work. This locomotive, and

Union Pacific's massive Challenger crosses the Clio viaduct (left) in California's Feather River Canyon. **ABOVE:** *The imposing front end of Union Pacific's No. 3985.*

844 too, exist for one reason only—to enhance the image and public presence of Union Pacific. These locomotives generate a lot of good will and favorable press and media attention, and a lot of employee pride and enthusiasm. That's why we have them—not because we think someday the steam engine will come back, because it never will, but for good business reasons. We use them only for commemorative and for very special events, not every county fair.

Union Pacific designed the 4-6-6-4 Challenger during the 1930s for hauling fast freights across the Great Plains and Rocky Mountains of the inland west. ALCO built 105 of them altogether. The first challenger was delivered in 1936 and the last, No. 3985 in 1943. Today, only No. 3985 survives in operating condition.

The Challengers were successful locomotives, but they lived up to their name—they were a real challenge to operate. Too big for many bridges and too long for some curves, they could be used only on about one-third of the vast UP trackage.

Challengers, like other extra-large locomotives, were far too long for a rigid frame. A hinged frame allowed them to "bend" when going around curves, providing observers with the thrill of watching the boiler swing out of its normal position, moving to the left or right. Such locomotives are called articulated. There are few still in existence, but Challenger is the

Back to the future, Southern Pacific style. There is only one of these cab-forwards left from SP's once-vast fleet, beautifully restored but not operating, at the California State Railroad Museum in Sacramento. The design helped keep the crews from being asphyxiated in the many long tunnels on SP's routes.

sole surviving operational example. It is not the biggest class of engine built in the United States, but it is big enough. At 121 feet (37m) long, it lists a total weight of more than one million pounds (454,000kg) when fully loaded and in working order. Although designed to consume coal, Number 3985 was converted to oil in 1990. The tender carries almost six thousand gallons (22,712l) of No. 5 fuel oil and twenty-five thousand gallons (94,635l) of water. Cylinders are twenty-one inches (53.5cm) by thirty-two inches (81cm) and are powered by 280 psi steam from the mammoth boiler.

S*P No. 3809 is a massive 2-8-8-4 Yellowstone type built by Lima Locomotive Works in 1939. Too big to restore, and too big to run on most of today's roadbed, nearly all of these were cut up in the 1950s.*

Another SP cab-forward (above) blasts past a rail fan from the 1950s, accelerating hard.

The Duluth, Missabe & Northern Railway's massive locomotives weren't built for speed or show, but to haul huge trailing loads of iron ore from mine to mill. No. 205 (right) is a 2-8-8-2, built in 1910 by Baldwin, shown here shortly before retirement in 1953.

R.M.&N.RY.
205

Steve Lee on Main Line Steam Operations

Union Pacific's Steve Lee steam program and its occasional main line excursions. Here he talks a bit about the challenges of taking the Challenger out on modern rails.

Rolling the Challenger out onto the main line is no easy task. Steve Lee, who runs Union Pacific's steam program and its occasional Main Line excursions, likens it to trying to drive a Model T Ford on the interstate. "You try to fit into traffic as best you can," he explains, "but these locomotives have some unique requirements." Here he talks about some of them.

One reason the railroads got rid of steam locomotives was that crewmen had to stop fairly often—to apply grease, to fuel and water, and for other essential maintenance. People who wish the railroads would go back to steam power just don't appreciate the tremendous amount of time and effort these machines require; the entire railroad system would be gridlocked and bankrupt if we tried.

It takes us months or even a year of preplanning to take the Challenger or 844 out for a trip, to keep the disruption of normal freight traffic to a minimum. These are big, heavy locomotives. There are lots of places where you can't take them—there's no place to turn them around, or they are too long to go around curves, or too heavy for some bridges. Diesel locomotives are heavy and big all right, but not like these locomotives! Size and weight were problems with steam locomotives; to do the work, they had to be big; so big, they ultimately outgrew their track structure. The Challenger, for example, was used by Union Pacific on only about one-third of the railroad; it was too big for the rest of the system. We have to keep that limitation in mind when we preplan a trip; we look at curvature, bridges, and switches. There are lots of places that might be nice to take the locomotive, but if you can't get there or can't turn the engine around to come home, the idea is moot.

In the old days, these things would run 150 or two hundred miles in a day, then go to a roundhouse to be serviced and inspected and repaired. Now we go out for weeks at a time! This thing isn't going to a shop until we get back, so it has to be in tip-top shape when it leaves here. And we also have to be prepared for the unexpected; that's why wherever this engine goes, we have a tool car right behind it with every conceivable spare part, plus tools for making the ones that were inconceivable. Something is going to bend or break or fall off, and you've got to be able to fix it on the spot! That begins with maintaining it in excellent condition, but you've got to be prepared for Murphy's Law.

Only Union Pacific has invested the time and effort to preserve much of the real heritage of mainline steam. Mixing a huge, old, complicated, somewhat fragile piece of machinery like this Big Boy in with modern diesel traffic is risky, expensive, difficult—and a delight to all who get to see it.

Union Pacific steam excursions are rare events, but they are booked solid. Here is the Big Boy climbing Telocaset Hill, near Union Junction, Oregon, with two spare tenders and UP diesel No. 3785 providing moral support.

Union Pacific No. 3985	
Length overall, including tender	121 feet 11 inches (37m)
Weight, in working order	1,071,000 pounds (486,234kg)
Boiler pressure	280psi
Drivers	69 inches (175cm)
Maximum tractive effort	97,350 pounds (44,197kg)
Grate area	132 square feet (12.3 sq m)
Tubes	45 2.5-inch (6.4cm) tubes; Tubes 177 4-inch (10.2m) tubes
Fuel type and capacity	Oil, #5 grade, 5,945 gallons (22,504l)
Heated surface area	4,642 square feet (431.7sqm)
Cylinder bore x stroke	21 inches by 32 inches (53.5×81cm)

DIXIANA
ROARING CAMP
&
BIG TREES

Chapter 9

Getting in Gear: Little Engines That Could

The ugly ducklings of the steam locomotive world must be the little Heislers, Climaxes, and Shays, geardrive logging locomotives designed for special duties to be performed at slow speeds and obscure rights of way.

A surprising number of these little engines have survived and remain in service, a testament to the durability of their robust design and perhaps the limited value of their scrap iron potential.

SHAY'S NEW WORKHORSE

Ephraihm Shay was a Michigan lumberman during the 1870s. He designed a small, specialized locomotive for use in the deep woods, suitable for hauling logs on rough temporary track. Conventional locomotives, with their large drivers, tore up the rail and often derailed. Shay's concept used a long horizontal driveshaft connected to powered trucks at the front and rear of the locomotive. Bevel gears instead of crank rods transmitted power from the driveshaft to the trucks. Comparatively tiny wheels helped keep the machine on track.

Shay commissioned the Lima Locomotive Works to build his prototype. Although it went only 15 miles per hour (24kph), the Shay locomotive stayed on the

*R**oaring Camp's star performer is this sturdy little Shay (**left**), freshly rebuilt and able to leap tall mountains at a single, very slow, bound.*
ABOVE: Exposed gears, Roaring Camp Shay.

rough rails and scampered up steep grades with heavy loads of cut timber.

These little locomotives were perfect for logging at a time when logging was a very big business. Three variations on the Shay design evolved, all featuring a horizontal shaft that drove powered swiveling trucks at both the front and rear of the locomotive. The patented Shay system used vertical cylinders at the rear of the boiler. The similar Climax machine put the cylinders near their normal locations, but at an incline, attached to a gearbox amidships. The Heisler was built around a V-2 cylinder arrangement, with two driveshafts powering the leading and trailing trucks.

STEAMING GEARDRIVE SURVIVORS

Two major tourist railroads still operate these charming little lumber locomotives: the Roaring Camp & Big Trees Railroad in the mountains south of San Francisco, and Cass Scenic Railroad Park in West

Virginia. Both lines feature steep grades through wonderful terrain.

The Shay was the dominant geared locomotive; 2,771 were built, most around 1900. They are compact, short, and slow. The drivetrain on the Shay is very reminiscent of that on a car or truck, only without the transmission. Vertical cylinders turn a crankshaft and the crankshaft turns a driveshaft through massive universal joints. Massive bevel gears drive the powered axles at the front and rear of the locomotive.

Dixiana, owned by the Roaring Camp Railroad, is a good example of the breed. Built in 1912 by Lima, she is a forty-ton (36t), oil-burning, two-truck Shay built for thirty-six-inch-gauge (91.5cm) track. Ninety years of labor haven't diminished Dixiana's ability to do a day's work; she regularly hauls six cars of tourists up four and a half miles (7.2km) of 8 percent grade, winding around twenty-six-degree curves far too tight for conventional locomotives.

ROARING CAMP

Roaring Camp claims to be the steepest narrow-gauge railroad in the United States, with an 8.5-percent grade on most of the line, and 9 percent on the switchback. That kind of work is very hard on the engines. The Shays do it well; they were built for steep grades and sharp curves. With six cars full of 150-pound (68kg) people, they are pulling a trailing load of about fifty tons (45t), and that's about what these locomotives were expected to do on those grades.

As Dan Ranger reports, "When you go around a switchback, where the angle of the boiler suddenly changes, and you are blow-torching up the mountain, you'd better have a fireman who knows what he's doing or you can have a catastrophic explosion in a real hurry! I'd rather have

*Steam vents from the Shay's cylinders (**left**), warming them before operation.*
RIGHT: *Climax No. 10, ready to roll. The pistons are mounted at an angle, rather than in the vertical position of the Shay.*

*Pistons, Roaring Camp No. 1 (**far left**). Steam is vented through the pistons for an hour or so before operation, bringing the steel and iron up to working temperature before the locomotive is moved. **LEFT:** The geardrive train isn't suitable for high speed but provides excellent torque and is very tolerant of the rough roadbeds common to logging and mining operations.*

Dan Ranger on the Shay

A former Southern Pacific fireman. Shares his thoughts on the Shay.

Former Southern Pacific fireman Dan Ranger has long been fascinated by the Shay. "To my way of thinking," says Ranger, "they are a lot easier to run and to work on than the Climax or Heisler. Everything's exposed and easy to work on. And when you're running a Shay, the valve gear is standing up on end, so that makes these components very well balanced." Here are some of the reasons why he likes these little gear-driven locomotives.

Unlike other engines, you can adjust the Johnson bar of a Shay with one hand. You wouldn't dare do that with a Heisler when it's working hard, or it will yank the bar right out of your hand. In fact, somebody once called the Heisler a "thrashing" machine, and I think that's accurate.

Shays always were, and still are, a pleasure to work on. They are very responsive. Because they are geared, and because they are slow, you can do things with them you couldn't do with a rod engine; it would slip right out from underneath you. A Shay is a lot more forgiving.

The Shay locomotives are quite durable. For example, we were working on Roaring Camp's Number 1 "Dixiana" and decided to replace the truck pedestals a couple of years ago. The castings had been repaired so many times that we elected to make new ones. A young man working in the shop looked at the old pedestals and said, "Lima sure didn't make very good castings!"

"How in the world can you say that?" I asked him. "If you had walked into the Lima shop back in 1912 when they were assembling this locomotive, and told them that this engine would still be running in 1994, you would have been hauled away in a straightjacket!" Nobody expected these locomotives to last more than about twenty years. They were the equivalent of a contractor's dump truck today, something to be used up and discarded when they wore out. They were expected to do the job, without a lot of maintenance. Nobody expected these engines to last a hundred years, as some of ours have.

I've fired both coal and oil locomotives. Like every other engine, a lot depends on how well they are set up and run. Either can be easy or hard. If a Shay is set up well when it is designed, it is likely to be a good steamer.

There are tricks to all of them—when I was firing back in North Carolina, the engineer had been on that locomotive since 1925. He taught me its tricks. One was that it liked a nice "heel" of coal across the back of the firebox, with coal scattered across the rest of the grate. And he was right; she did fine! That was also true of the old K36s I used to fire in New Mexico; most liked a good "horseshoe" bank of coal across the back of the grate. If you keep that in good order, most will be happy. All except for the old Number 484—I never could fire it properly, I never learned her tricks. Number 489 was a sweetheart. I mentioned that to her engineer one day. He said, "Sure you have a good time firing that locomotive. My cat could fire 489!"

Oil burners are different. For one thing, you have to pay closer attention to whatever the engineer is doing. You can regulate the oil a lot quicker than you can with coal. Once the coal is in the firebox, you can't turn it off.

I can remember firing an engine on the Southern Pacific, Number 2717, that liked cold oil! The standard way to check the proper temperature of the Bunker C fuel oil was to put the back of your hand against the feed line. If it was uncomfortably warm, it was about the right temperature. Bunker C at room temperature is like jelly, almost solid. But warmed up, it is fine.

So the one and only time I fired the engine, I came in on the afternoon shift. The oil was kind of cold, so I turned on the tank heater and got it warmed up. I fired it that day and had a miserable time!

When I got off it at midnight, the other fireman asked, "You didn't heat the oil in this thing, did you?" I told him I had.

"Oh, I'm in for a rough night tonight!" he said. "The line heater on this one leaks if the oil always gets warmed up. If you warm it in the tank it gets overheated and doesn't burn right!" Well, nobody told me about it. Those are the kinds of tricks you learn about individual locomotives!

somebody working who's scared and nervous during the running and firing than somebody who puts his feet up and thinks his job is a piece of cake. It's true of rail line that has a decent grade; you better know where you are with your water supply or you're in big trouble!"

COG DRIVING UP MT. WASHINGTON

One radical variation on the geardrive locomotive can still be found at the Mt. Washington, New Hampshire, Cog Railway. Mt. Washington is the tallest point in New England. Elevation at the top is 6,288 feet (1,916.5m) and it has long been a tourist attraction. One building on the summit, the Tip Top House, dates to 1852.

Sylvester Marsh created a three-mile-long (4.8km) railroad to take visitors to the top of the mountain in 1869. The Mt. Washington line was the first such mountain-climbing railroad in the world and now remains as the last coal-fired steam line of that type.

The average grade for the line is 25 percent and the ruling grade is a staggering 37.4 percent. The grade is so steep that specialized design details were required. Simple adhesion doesn't work on grades that steep, so Mt. Washington's locomotives use cogs—drivegears instead of driving wheels. The gear meshes with a series of cogs anchored to the center of the track, pulling the locomotive and its consist up the steep grade, slowly but surely.

Conventional boiler placement does not work on such grades either, so the Cog Railway locomotives all look as though they've been in wrecks: the boilers angle down at a steep, strange-looking tilt. The steepest part of the line is a stretch called Jacob's Ladder. At this point, passengers in the front of the coaches are fourteen feet (4.3m) higher than those in the rear!

Mt. Washington maintains seven cog locomotives, some dating to the 1870s. None is fast; three or four miles per hour (4.8–6.5kph) is normal.

All locomotives, including the little geardrive models, have extensive collections of accessories (left)—air compressors, electrical generators, injectors, feed water heaters.

Eccles Valley Lumber Company's Shay (above) performing at the Sumpter Valley Railroad in Oregon. The big balloon stack helps control the fire hazard from sparks and cinders, a major problem for logging operations.

2860
BRITISH COLUMBIA
2860

Chapter 10

A Very Royal Hudson

The 4-6-4 locomotive didn't make its appearance on the North American stage until 1925. The first apparently was designed for Chicago, Milwaukee & St. Paul, but the railroad went out of business before the locomotive could be built. New York Central acquired the first 4-6-4 to be completed in 1927 and named the new beast in honor of its Hudson River route.

This first 4-6-4, NYC No. 5300, was tested and found quite successful for the heavy passenger train consists of the day. Another fifty-nine were promptly ordered, and many more after that. Within a few years, NYC alone had more than two hundred Hudsons.

Steam locomotive history and heritage are revered north of the border just as much as in the United States, but with a distinctly Canadian flavor and style. The best example of that flavor is BC Rail's wonderful Royal Hudson, perhaps the most beautiful and hardworking contemporary passenger steam locomotive.

BC Rail runs the Royal Hudson on a daily eighty-mile (129km) round trip from Vancouver up the Howe Sound to the town of Squamish, with the beautiful British Columbia coast on one side of the train and dramatic mountains on the other. The trip takes six hours and tends to be booked solid; reservations are required.

T*his elegant creature (left) is BC Rail's famous Royal Hudson, and it is still in regular scheduled service.* **ABOVE:** *Detail from Canada's Pacific's No. 2860.*

BC Rail No. 2860 wasn't born royal. Instead, she was part of the last batch of Hudsons purchased by Canadian Pacific. Sixty-five of these handsome locomotives were built, the first in 1929 and the last in 1940, by Montreal Locomotive Works. Five variants of the basic design were used, designated H1a through H1e; No. 2860 is one of the last, an "e" model, and the first one of the last group of five built for Canadian Pacific.

CP used the Hudson for both passenger and freight service, with great success. With top speeds of better than 90mph (145kph), No. 2860 and her sisters scampered across the broad Canadian prairie provinces and up and over the Rockies.

These locomotives all shared the same basic specifications: ninety feet, ten inches (27.5m) long (including tender); fifteen feet, six inches high (4.8m); seventy-five-inch (190.5cm) drivers; and cylinders twenty-two inches (56cm) by thirty inches (76cm). With working boilers rated at

275psi, the CP Hudsons applied 42,250 pounds (19,182kg) of effort to the drawbar, about forty-five hundred hp at 60mph (97kph). A booster truck provides about 10 percent more power at low speeds and kicks out at 21mph (38kph).

Locomotives of this size need fuel at rates faster than their firemen can shovel, so this entire class of Hudson has automatic stokers. All were originally coal-fired.

Although the basics stayed the same throughout the production run, there were some variants in these locomotives. The first twenty were fairly clunky-looking engines, similar in appearance to most others in service: their pilots were made from recycled boiler tubes, they all had obvious steam and sand domes, and all had visible feed water heaters attached.

The second batch of forty-five got some streamlining and a polished steel jacket, painted black to give a more aerodynamic look.

It was the final group that got the royal treatment. Features included a solid pilot, smoke deflectors, and a hidden stack, a sleek boiler without visible domes for steam or sand. The headlight was set flush with the front of the smoke box. Instead of the ordinary basic black, these locomotives emerged from the factory with maroon paint, gold trim, and white wheels.

George VI of England and Elizabeth visited Canada in 1939, and one of the Hudsons, No. 2850, was selected to pull the royal train westbound from Quebec to Vancouver, a trip of 3,224 miles (5187.5km). She was repainted just for the occasion in royal blue with polished aluminum trim, with a crown added to the front of each footboard to indicate her royal assignment.

The trip went off without a hitch. Crews were changed twenty-five times during the run across Canada, but the handsome Hudson remained "power on the

Canadian Pacific No. 2317 provided sightseeing services for Canadian rail fans, halting here at Scranton, Pennsylvania. **FOLLOWING PAGES:** No. 2816 on another excursion trip, stopping here at Bellowsville, Vermont.

PULLMAN
CANADIAN PACIFIC
2816

Canadian Pacifics No. 2860

Al Broadfoot, of BC Rail, comments on their last Hudson.

BC Rail in Northen Vancouver is the proud owner of Canadian Pacific's Royal Hudson No. 2860. Here, BC's Al Broadfoot comments on the beautiful locomotive, which still runs daily.

CP Rail was noted for the fine lines of its locomotives. Number 2860 was one of five designed specifically for service in British Columbia, working the run from Vancouver to Revelstoke. They were oil-burners because of the forest fire hazard from coal-burning locomotives. When they were introduced, the Hudsons were the first locomotives able to run the entire division without having to refuel.

All the lines were blown out and the accessories repaired and running, and the boiler was retubed. That was all that was done to 2860 before it went back in service. Retubing the locomotive ended up costing as much as the price of the whole locomotive when it was new!

She's been very successful generally. We run her during the summer, then do our maintenance work during the winter. I've rebuilt the Hudson twice now. Like any steam locomotive, the minute it starts to move, it begins wearing out. The Hudson, like all steam locomotives, is very labor-intensive and expensive to operate. Without changing the appearance of the locomotive, I have modified some things to make it more efficient. I've replaced the friction bearings on the leading and trailing trucks, and on the tender, and added more grease fittings. It is currently a very well maintained locomotive, probably better than during its working days for CP Rail. The railroads used to push these locomotives hard for five years, then send them in for overhaul when they were completely worn out. When I got this engine, it was junk! The bushings were so bad that they were worn an inch into the frame!

But now we keep the Hudson right up to standard. It is federally and provincially certified. Both our steam engines are certified to run anywhere in North America, a rarity on some railroads like Burlington Northern.

But the Hudson has become something of an icon to the Canadian railroad industry now. [It] is the only "time card" passenger steam engine running in North America, and we probably run more often than any other steamer, four months a year, plus charters.

American locomotives tend to have a cluttered look; they are a plumber's nightmare, but these Hudsons have a clean appearance. A lot of their piping is hidden out of the way. Only five were really streamlined, but all had a nice clean look to them. All sixty-five Hudsons were very successful for CP. They ran them eighty, ninety, or one hundred miles per hour (129–161kph) all the time.

Canadian Pacific Royal Hudson No. 2860	
Length overall, including tender	not available
Weight, in working order	657,500 pounds (298,505kg)
Boiler pressure	275psi
Drivers	75 inches (190.5cm)
Maximum tractive effort	45,200 pounds (20,521kg); 57,250 (25,992kg) with booster
Grate area	80.8 square feet (7.5 sq m)
Tubes	58 2.25-inch (5.7cm) tubes, 17 3.5-inch (8.9cm) flues
Fuel type and capacity	Oil, 4,000 gallons (15,142l)
Heated surface area	3,791 square feet (352.6 sq m)
Cylinder bore x stroke	22 inches by 30 inches (56x76cm)

B.C. Rail's Hudson (opposite) chuffs out of Vancouver, the last scheduled steam passenger service in action, and certainly one of the most attractive operational engines in North America.

point" for the whole trip. Afterward, No. 2850 was repainted maroon and went back to more conventional assignments. CP, however, asked for permission to keep the crowns and the designation "royal" for the locomotive to commemorate her exemplary service to the king. Both requests were granted, and in fact all the Hudsons from this class owned by CP were so designated. No. 2850 survives and is on display in Delson, Quebec, at the Railway Museum. The coaches used by the royals during this trip also survive at the National Science Museum in Ottawa.

CP No. 2860 was the first of the Hudsons delivered after the royal visit, the first new Royal Hudson. She was delivered in 1940 and steamed through the World War II years and into the middle 1950s, until diesels took over. During her career, she hauled trains between Vancouver and Revelstoke, a difficult run through mountainous terrain. She labored a while on the Kettle Valley Railway, too, but by 1955, CP Rail didn't need steam engines any longer. The Royal Hudsons, despite their little crowns, went to the dead line, consigned to be cut up for scrap.

No. 2860 barely escaped the torch. She was stored in Winnipeg, missing some of her accessories, waiting for the inevitable, when CP was approached by a small group of rail fans. This group bought No. 2860 for seven thousand dollars (Canadian). The bell had been "liberated" by someone who didn't want to see it melted down; it was returned when the locomotive was saved. In 1964 a proposed rail museum attempted a restoration project. The museum idea collapsed but No. 2860 managed to survive. Finally, the government of British Columbia bought her in 1974, managed to get her serviceable, and put her back on track. No. 2860 became the only steam locomotive in regular main line service, a distinction she retains to this day.

RECREATION AND RESOURCES

There are about fourteen hundred steam locomotives in existence in the United States and Canada. About three hundred of these engines are functional, operated mostly by museums, tourist attractions, and volunteer historic preservation groups. In addition, the Union Pacific Railroad has a very active steam program featuring its Challenger and its never-retired No. 844 Northern.

Each of these groups has something different to offer. Some, like the Smithsonian in Washington, D.C., and the California State Railroad Museum in Sacramento, have wonderful artifacts and displays. Those museums are free but have a strict "don't touch" policy; their locomotives will never move again. Others, like the many tourist lines, allow you to observe working steam at a distance and at a cost, from a passenger car behind a steam locomotive. The preservation groups often have only one or two locomotives, sometimes in parts scattered around a drafty engine house, but here you will be able to actually get your hands on an engine. You'll get filthy dirty while cleaning and polishing mystery chunks of cast iron and steel, and perhaps serve an apprenticeship to learn to become a fireman or engineer. And finally there are some groups that will, for a price, give you a short course in steam locomotive operation and allow you to take the throttle for a little well-supervised spin.

The following list includes just a few selected suggested resources of all kinds, based on the prejudices and preferences of the author.

BC Rail

BC Rail's Royal Hudson No. 2860 is certainly one of the most beautiful steam locomotives in operation today, and one of the most popular. A six-hour, eighty-mile (129km) round trip through spectacular British Columbian scenery is well worth the forty-six-dollar (Canadian) adult fare. Reservations are required for the trip along Howe Sound to the little town of Squamish, where the Royal Hudson pauses for a two-hour layover, then returns to Vancouver. *1311 West First Street, North Vancouver, BC, V6B 4XS Canada; (800) 663-8238*

California State Railroad Museum

This is one of the major railroad museums in the nation, and is housed right at the western end of the transcontinental railroad in Old Sacramento, California. With twenty-one restored locomotives, including the only cab-forward, plus a reasearch library and frequent excursion events, this is a real treat for rail fans and just about anybody else. *111 I Street, Old Sacramento, CA, 95814*

Cass Scenic Railroad State Park

Cass is another short line tourist operation, famous for its little geared ex-logging locomotives and scenic terrain. Cass and Roaring Camp both claim to have the steepest grades and both operate Shays, but Cass is a standard-gauge line whereas Roaring Camp is narrow-gauge. *Box 107, Cass, WV 24927; (304) 456-4300 or (800) CALL-WVA; email: cassrr@ neumedia.net*

Golden Gate Railroad Museum

Rail fans in the San Francisco Bay area can visit the Golden Gate Railroad Museum, tucked away inside the old Hunter's Point Naval Shipyard facility in San Francisco. Here you can watch several old locomotives and many railcars undergoing rebuilds and maintenance and even pitch in to help as a volunteer. *PO Box 881686, San Francisco, California 94188; (415) 822-8739*

Nevada Northern

Nevada Northern is a perfectly preserved, not restored, old railroad tucked away in one of the most remote places in the United States. Its fine old Baldwin ten-wheeler is available for rental and instruction. Scheduled excursions depart from a well-preserved old depot, and when the train chugs past the "red light" district in Ely, the "girls" come out of the bordellos to wave at the tourists and display their ample wares. The old shops, depot, freight house and engine house are all pretty much just the way they were when the line shut down, many years ago. Well worth the drive. *East Ely Depot, 1100 Avenue A, East Ely, NV 89315; (702) 289-2085*

Nevada State Railroad Museum

Nevada is a great place to see authentic steam locomotives in a Western locale, and one of the most interesting collections is at the Nevada State Railroad Museum in the old silver mining boom town of Carson City. Headquartered in a new facility near the center of town, the building and exhibit demonstrate the commitment of the state of Nevada to preserve its unique railroad heritage. This fine collection of well-preserved and operating locomotives, available for inspection, is from the narrow-gauge Virginia & Truckee Railroad. This is probably the best collection of classic early wood-burning locomotives of the 4-4-0 American Standard type still in working condition. Steam operations are typically scheduled on alternate weekends from May through September, plus one weekend in October and one in December. Be sure to call or write for current information and directions to the site. *Capitol Complex, Carson City, NV 89710; (702) 687-6953*

Roaring Camp & Big Trees Narrow Gauge Railroad

Tucked into the tall redwood trees above San Jose and Silicon Valley in California, the old Roaring Camp & Big Trees operates three little old logging locomotives in a beautiful setting. Three little geared locomotives are used here, two Shays and an 1899 Heisler. The line runs up the steepest narrow-gauge line in North America to the top of Bear Mountain, pauses long enough for lunch, and returns. Write or call for a schedule and current fares. *PO Box G-1, Felton, CA 95018; (408) 335-4484*

Smithsonian Institution

Even though the Smithsonian collection doesn't include working steam, a visit to the Railroad Hall in the Museum of History and Technology on the Mall in Washington, D.C. is a treat for anybody who loves locomotives. Many of the earliest and most important steam locomotives in America are beautifully presented. Admission is free and the Smithsonian is open daily from 10 A.M. until 5:30 P.M. *14th Street and Constitution Avenue, Washington, DC 20560; (202)357-2700*

Steamtown National Historic Site

Steamtown is a fairly new museum operated by the National Park Service and dedicated to the celebration of steam locomotive operation. The place is much cleaner and tidier than any working engine house during the steam era, but otherwise the place has a lot to offer: three functional locomotives, lots of displays and exhibits, tours of the roundhouse and shops, and a twenty-seven-mile (43.5km) roundtrip excursion from Scranton to Moscow, Pennsylvania. The museum uses the old shops and roundhouse of the Delaware, Lackawanna & Western Railroad. Open daily year round from 9:00 A.M. to 5:00 P.M. except for Thanksgiving, Christmas, and New Year's Day.

150 South Washington Avenue, Scranton, PA 18503; (717) 340-5200

Valley Railroad's Essex Steam Train and Riverboat Ride

Valley Railroad runs along the Connecticut River, a beautiful and unspoiled bit of New England within easy travel of New York and the other major metropolitan regions of the Northeast. "Power on the point" is normally the handsome and well-maintained No. 40, a small Mikado. Trips last two and a half hours and most connect with a riverboat cruise at Deep River. Valley operates daily from May through October, weekends in November and December. Call or write for more information.

PO Box 452, Essex, CT 06426; (860) 767-0103

STOCK PHOTOGRAPHY

Most of the photography in this book is available for editorial and advertising applications at normal stock photography rates. For further information contact Stock Photo Sales at Military Stock Photography, 240 South 13th Street, San Jose, California 95112 U.S.A.

SELECTED BIBLIOGRAPHY

Steam locomotive reference works are numerous and sometimes contradictory. In addition to specific data provided by owners of locomotives described in this book, my primary sources for technical data have been:

Conrad, J. David. Steam Locomotive Directory of North America, Railroad Reference Number 8. 2 vols. Kalmbach Publishing, 1987.

Drury, George, ed. *Guide to North American Steam Locomotives*. Kalmbach Publishing, 1993.

Hollingsworth, Brian. *Illustrated Encyclopedia of the World's Steam Passenger Locomotives*. Crescent Books, 1983.

White, John H., Jr. *A History of the American Locomotive: Its Development: 1830-1880*. Johns Hopkins Press, 1980.

PHOTO CREDITS

©Howard Ande: p. 90

©Hans Halberstadt: pp. 6–7, 12–13, 31, 33, 34, 41, 44, 52–53 both, 54, 58, 102–103 both, 104, 106–107 both, 109 bottom

Collection of Hans Halberstadt: pp. 8–9, 20, 22–23, 24, 28–29 both, 30–31, 36–37, 42–43, 45, 46–47, 48 both, 49, 65 bottom, 72–73, 74–75, 78–79 both, 83, 88–89 both, 94–95 both, 96–97 both, 101 sidebar, 104–105, 109 top, 110–111, 116 sidebar; ©Peter Eurlich: pp. 18–19, back endpapers; ©FoleyFotos: pp. 26–27, 112–113, 114–115, front endpapers; ©Grant L. Ferguson: pp. 111, 117; GGRM Collection: pp. 73, 74; ©Grayson Rail Photos: p. 25; ©J. L. Haugh: pp. 16–17; ©Don Jilson: p. 86; ©Dennis Schmidt: pp. 32–33

©Brian Solomon: pp. 2, 10–11 both, 14, 15, 17, 19, 21, 22, 35, 38, 39, 40–41, 50–51 both, 54–55, 56, 57, 59, 60–61 both, 62–63 both, 64, 65 top, 66, 67 both, 68–69 both, 70–71 both, 76–77, 80–81 both, 82–83, 84–85 both, 87, 91, 92–93 both, 98–99, 100–101